MIND
BLOWN!

13-Digit ISBN: 978-1-40035-302-6
10-Digit ISBN: 1-40035-302-5

Books published by Cider Mill Press Book Publishers are available at special discounts for bulk purchases in the United States by corporations, institutions, and other orga- nizations. For more information, please contact the publisher.

Applesauce Press is an imprint of Cider Mill Press Book Publishers

"Where good books are ready for press"

501 Nelson Place
Nashville, Tennessee 37214, USA

cidermillpress.com

HarperCollins Publishers, Macken House, 39/40 Mayor Street Upper,
Dublin 1, D01 C9W8, Ireland (https://www.harpercollins.com)

Illustrations by Diego Vaisberg

Background patterns and line drawings used under official license from Shutterstock.

Printed in Malaysia

25 26 27 28 29 PJM 5 4 3 2 1

First Edition

MIND BLOWN!

THE ULTIMATE SCIENCE BOOK FOR CURIOUS KIDS

250+ AMAZING FACTS
ABOUT SPACE, ANIMALS, HUMAN BIOLOGY, AND MORE!

SHANE CARLEY

APPLESAUCE PRESS

For Parker Carley
(and all the other
curious kids out there)

CONTENTS

INTRODUCTION

Did you know you can taste garlic with your feet? Or that comets smell like rotten eggs? Prepare to have your mind blown! This book is packed with more than 250 incredible science facts about the human body, plants and animals, outer space, technology, physics, chemistry, and more that will shock and amaze you.

Examining the world around us through a scientific lens can lead to some pretty awesome discoveries. It can take us deep inside ourselves to explain how our bodies work. It can take us to the far reaches of outer space, giving us tools to learn about stars, galaxies, and black holes. That scientific lens can inspire us to examine the plants and animals living around us. It can even help us invent things so incredible, they sometimes seem like magic.

Some facts may seem stranger than any fiction you've ever read . . . but the truth is here for you to discover! So, dive in and discover how a hurricane forms or how much you'd weigh on another planet. Meet the man who came up with the theory of evolution and the women who helped America win the space race.

Buckle up and hold on tight. It's time to get *Mind Blown*!

HUMAN BIOLOGY

Human biology may sound like a stuffy subject, but there's nothing stuffy about these incredible facts about the human body. Your body is like a well-oiled machine. Everything inside you has a purpose and function, no matter how weird or wacky it seems!

Can you guess how many times your heart will beat in your lifetime? More than 2 billion! Do you know you were born with more bones than you'll have when you're an adult? What would you do if I told you that thousands of mites are living inside the pores on your face right now?! (Don't panic—they're good mites!)

Find out who "the dark lady of DNA" is, whether or not your DNA is part Neanderthal, and what to say the next time someone claims that sugar makes you hyper.

Are you ready? Hang on to your head!

Fact or Fiction?

The average human produces enough saliva in their lifetime to fill a bathtub more than 50 times.

Your salivary glands are active most of the time, which means they're almost always making saliva.

Fact!

Scientists say the average human produces 720 milliliters of saliva (better known as *spit*) each day—enough to fill just over two soda cans! That means in one year we make a little more than 260 liters of spit. Just imagine walking into a grocery store and seeing a long row of soda bottles filled with your saliva—130 bottles of it! If you live to be 80 years old, you'll have produced more than 20,000 liters of spit. That's enough to fill your bathtub 50 times. Yuck!

But as gross as saliva can be, it actually plays a very big role for humans and other animals. If you've ever had a dry mouth, you know how bad it feels. Spit keeps your mouth moist, which helps you chew, swallow, and break down food more easily. It also helps keep your teeth healthy and (believe it or not) plays a role in preventing bad breath. Turns out spit is pretty important stuff!

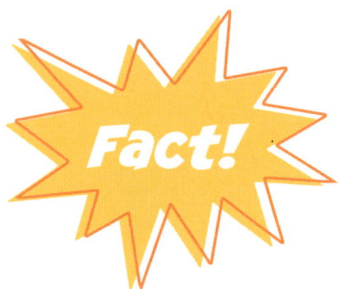

Your nose and ears will never stop growing.

Sometimes elderly people seem to have large ears and noses, which led to the myth that those parts of the body never stop growing. In reality, your nose and ears are mostly made of cartilage, and cartilage *definitely* doesn't grow forever. But cartilage is softer than bone. That means gravity can pull on your cartilage more than it can pull on other parts of your body.

Fiction!

Even though ears and noses stop growing, over time they might keep getting longer from that gravitational pull. So your ears and nose might keep getting longer over time . . . even if they've already stopped growing! And according to doctors, other parts of the body (like lips and cheeks) tend to grow *smaller* over time, which can make drooping noses and sagging earlobes look even larger. But don't worry—this is all just a natural part of the aging process.

If you really want to escape the effects of gravity, you could always think about moving to space!

Try It!

Want to feel tall? Measure yourself in the morning.

Humans are actually taller in the morning than at night. Why? Gravity compresses your spine throughout the day, making you slightly shorter. When you lie down to sleep, that pressure eases, allowing your spinal fluid to help your spine recover. Try it: Measure your height in the morning and again at night. The difference is small (about half an inch), but it's real!

Astronauts in zero gravity don't have that spinal compression. Instead of shrinking they actually grow taller—sometimes by over an inch during long space missions. Of course, once back on Earth, gravity pulls them back down to normal height. Still, pretty neat, right?

You (mostly) breathe through one nostril at a time. Try this and see what happens!

Breathe on a mirror. You'll see more fog from one nostril than the other. That's because one nostril does about 75% of the work at a time, while the other takes a break. Every few hours, they switch. It's called the nasal cycle, and it helps your nose stay clear, moist, and better protected from dust and other irritants. Cool, huh?

Some people can taste colors.

People with a condition called synesthesia experience the world in a unique way. Their senses kind of work in overdrive!

Synesthesia can take many different forms. For example, some people with synesthesia taste particular flavors when they see colors or words. Others might feel tingling or see colors or shapes when they hear certain sounds. Some people even have a reaction when they see certain numbers or patterns.

Many famous writers and artists have synesthesia. Because of this, the way they experience the world often comes through in their art in interesting ways.

Weird But True!

When you lose weight, you breathe most of it out.

Studies have shown that when humans break down fat during weight loss, 84% of it turns into carbon dioxide and leaves the body through the lungs. That's right—when you lose weight, you're literally exhaling fat!

The explanation is actually pretty simple. When fat breaks down, it has to go somewhere. The process of "burning" fat creates waste products—in this case, carbon dioxide and water. Fortunately, your body already has a pair of organs that are very good at getting rid of carbon dioxide: your lungs! The water, on the other hand, usually makes its way to your bladder and leaves your body when you use the bathroom.

Your stomach acid is strong enough to dissolve metal.

The acid in your stomach is hydrochloric acid—the same strong acid that's sometimes used to process steel. It won't dissolve all metals, but scientists have found that stomach acid will cause certain metals to break down over time. However, the things you eat only stay in your stomach for an hour or two, which isn't enough time for the acid to work its magic on *actual* metal. Not that you would ever eat metal in the first place! (Definitely don't do that.)

You have thousands of mites living on your face right now.

Don't panic! Demodex mites are microscopic creatures that are sometimes called eyelash mites. They live inside your pores and eat the greasy oil your skin makes to keep from drying out. That means demodex mites are actually pretty helpful. Without them, your skin would be dirty and oily!

It's a little weird to think about thousands of tiny creatures living on your face, but there's nothing to be afraid of. Demodex mites are completely harmless—your body doesn't even notice them. In very rare cases, if something unusual happens with your skin or immune system, they can cause problems—but for nearly everyone, they just hang out quietly, doing no harm at all. In fact, they're so harmless that the name *demodex* comes from the Greek words for "fat" and "boring worm."

You can prevent tooth decay by eating cheese.

Cheese isn't just delicious—it's dentist-recommended! Well, sort of.

Cheese contains a special protein called *casein* that actually coats your teeth, creating a protective barrier. Studies have shown that eating cheese at the end of a meal can help protect your enamel from the acids certain foods can leave in your mouth. That means cheese can actually strengthen your teeth and prevent tooth decay!

Having a "cheese course" at the end of a meal is common in certain countries. Who knew this tradition was also good for your health?

Fact or Fiction?

If you laid all your blood vessels end to end, they would wrap halfway around the world.

The actual length of your blood vessels is longer—like, *way* longer! The average human has more than 60,000 miles of blood vessels inside them. That means your blood vessels could wrap all the way around the surface of Earth—twice!

Fiction!

From your brain down to your toes, just about every part of your body needs blood. With so many veins, arteries, and capillaries carrying blood throughout your entire body, it's pretty cool that problems like clogs and blockages are still (relatively) rare. It turns out the human body is actually a pretty efficient machine!

The human body is as salty as seawater.

The human body has a lot of salt in it. If you've ever tasted your sweat or tears, you know they're slightly salty. In fact, about 0.4% of a human's body weight comes from salt. An average person who weighs 150 pounds has about 0.6 pounds of salt inside them! Now imagine a cup filled up to the top with salt.

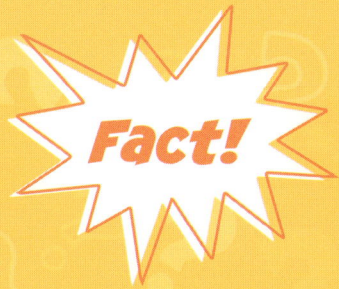

Fact!

The human body is constantly losing salt; therefore, we need to replace it on a regular basis. That's one reason why humans like to eat salty foods. A little salt is a good, healthy thing, but too much salt can be a problem. It can cause health issues like high blood pressure.

Since your body is constantly changing, giving it exactly what it needs isn't always easy. The key is to find a healthy balance!

HOW IT WORKS

Understanding "The Placebo Effect."

A placebo is a fake pill. It's made to look like a medicine pill, but it has no medicine in it. Placebos are often used in medical studies to help the experts figure out if a medicine is actually working. One group of participants gets the actual medicine: that's the experimental group. The other group gets a placebo pill. Then, researchers measure the different results between the two groups. One of the coolest things about this kind of experiment is that sometimes the people in the placebo group get better even though they aren't taking the real medicine! This is called the placebo effect and shows how powerful the human brain can be: just thinking you're taking medicine can actually improve your health! Most amazing of all, scientists have found that the placebo effect still happens, even if the person knows they're taking a placebo!

Of course, the placebo effect doesn't always work. It can't cure cancer or prevent heart disease. But for patients suffering with long-term pain, nausea, or other hard-to-measure conditions, the placebo effect can make a big difference. Some scientists have even proposed making "open-label" placebo pills available so patients can buy them themselves!

Humans are the only animals with a chin.

You might be thinking, *But I scratch my dog under his chin all the time.* Still, it's true. Other animals have a lower jaw, but only humans have a bone that sticks out to create a chin.

Why are humans so special that we deserve a chin? Scientists aren't quite sure. Some think having a chin helps us chew our food, while others think it plays a role in how we speak. Some scientists even say our chin has no purpose at all—it's just a random mutation that stuck around. Whatever the case, the chin is one of our most noticeable facial features. Enjoy it!

Your brain automatically ignores your nose.

Rude, but true! Close your left eye. You can see your nose, right? Now close your right eye. You should see your nose again. That's because your nose is between your eyes, which means it's always in your field of vision. So why don't you see your nose when both eyes are open?

The answer is that your brain automatically ignores it using a process called *unconscious selective attention.* Your nose would be a pretty big obstacle right smack in the middle of your vision. But since both of your eyes can see "around" your nose, your brain automatically fills in the gaps. If you really focus, you can see a sort of hazy outline where your nose should be—but if you aren't paying close attention, your brain completely filters it out. Pretty amazing, right?

There are people who can't actually feel pain.

It's true! A tiny percentage of humans are born without the ability to feel pain. That might sound like a super-power, but it can actually be a pretty big problem. People with this condition sometimes don't know when they hurt themselves, which means they might not realize they need to see a doctor. They need to carefully examine their bodies for scrapes, cuts, and other injuries just to make sure they're still in one piece! It would be nice to not feel pain when you stub your toe, but the condition makes everyday life a real hassle.

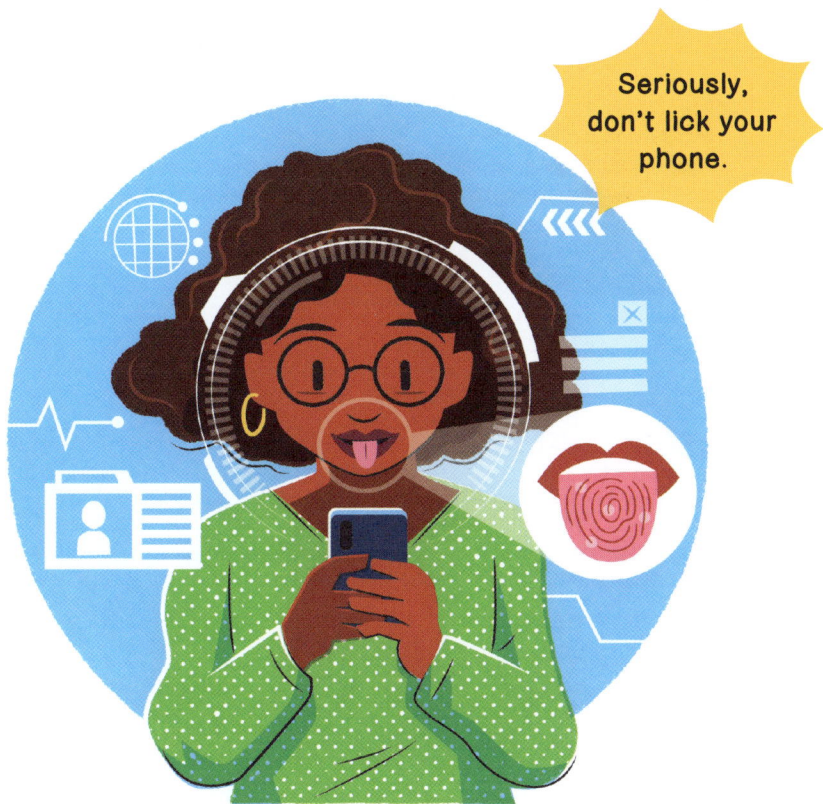

Seriously, don't lick your phone.

Your fingerprint isn't the only unique part of your body.

Every human has a unique fingerprint pattern. That's why you can unlock your phone using your fingerprint, and it's why the police make sure suspects provide a fingerprint sample. But did you know there are other parts of the body that are unique, too? Scientists have found that every human also has a unique tongue, and some have theorized that a "tongue print" might be just as reliable as voice recognition, facial recognition, and even fingerprints!

Of course, you probably won't be unlocking your phone with a tongue print anytime soon. Ew!

Fact or Fiction?

The dust in your home is mostly made from human skin.

For some reason, the myth that dust is made entirely from skin flakes has been making the rounds for a long time. While it's true that humans shed *a lot* of skin flakes over the course of the day, most of them tend to wind up in the shower drain.

Fiction!

Dust is known as an *allergen*, which means it can irritate your nose and make you cough and sneeze. Depending on the source, dust can even carry harmful chemicals. Most dust is actually tracked in from outside the house: It's made up of dirt, pollen, soot, and other particles that cling to your shoes and clothes whenever you go outside. Other things, like fibers from clothing and carpeting (or even pet hair), make up most of the rest.

So, don't worry: Dust may be gross, but it isn't *that* gross!

You have an organ in your body that can regenerate or regrow.

It's your liver, and it's a pretty amazing organ. It's the largest solid organ in the body, roughly the size of a football. The liver is super important: It cleans your blood, filtering out the toxins that leave your body when you use the bathroom. It also stores certain vitamins and minerals that your body needs to stay healthy.

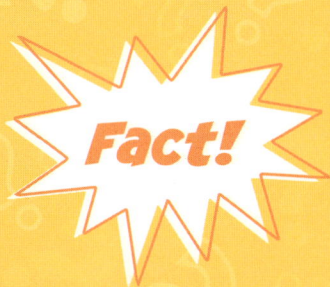

Fact!

But what's really amazing about the liver is its ability to heal itself. When other organs are damaged, they form scars. We see scars on skin after an injury or a surgery. The same thing happens with your other organs—except the liver. The liver can completely regenerate, replacing damaged cells with brand-new ones. In fact, the liver can regrow to its original size, even if 90% of it has been removed!

Because of the liver's incredible ability to regenerate, liver transplants are more flexible than other organ transplants. Doctors can even perform a partial liver transplant, where they remove a section of liver from a healthy living donor and implant it in a sick patient. Thanks to the liver's regenerative powers, both the donor's and recipient's livers will grow back to full size and function within just a few months. This makes liver transplants unique—they don't always require a full organ from a deceased donor like most transplants do. While the procedure is still complex, the option of living donors and the liver's natural ability to regrow make it more accessible and potentially faster than other transplants. Amazing!

1% of people have two different-colored eyes.

A small portion of the world's population has a condition called *heterochromia*, which causes their eyes to be two different colors. Sometimes this is easy to notice; for example, someone may have one blue eye and one hazel eye. Other times, heterochromia can be difficult to detect.

Heterochromia isn't common in humans, but it is in animals. For instance, white cats often have one blue eye and one yellow eye—you may have even noticed this yourself!

People read more slowly on a computer screen.

Researchers have repeatedly found that humans read and remember information printed on a page much better than information on a screen. They say humans read roughly 10 to 30% more slowly on a screen, and their ability to understand what they are reading drops as well. It's a headscratcher, all right. Scientists think screens create problems like eye strain, which changes the way your eyes receive information. The blue light emitted by screens can also make your eyes more tired, which makes reading harder. Long live the printed word!

Parts of your body have silly names.

Did you know that the area between your eyebrows and your nose is called the glabella? Or that the groove between your nose and your upper lip is called the philtrum? Or that the fleshy thing hanging down the back of your throat is called the uvula? Lots of body parts have silly-sounding scientific names—we just don't have a reason to use them very often! Even common body parts have scientific names you may not know. For instance, did you know your big toe is technically called your hallux? Or that your armpit is called the axilla? Next time you have the chance, throw one of these silly-sounding words into a conversation, and watch for any recognition from your audience. They'll think you're a real genius!

Rosalind Franklin: The Dark Lady of DNA

You've probably heard of DNA. It's a natural chemical in the body that carries instructions for how we look and function. DNA was first discovered by Swiss chemist Friedrich Miescher in 1869, but it took nearly 100 years for scientists to understand what it does and what it looks like. In 1951, chemist Rosalind Franklin began studying DNA using X-rays to photograph its

Rosalind Franklin

structure. Her photos revealed that DNA had a shape called a double helix. In 1953, scientists James Watson and Francis Crick used her findings to build the famous model of DNA's structure. In 1962, Watson, Crick, and Maurice Wilkins received the Nobel Prize for this discovery. Rosalind had died in 1958 at age 37, and the Nobel Prize isn't awarded after death. One of her photos, known as "Photo 51," gave key evidence for DNA's spiral shape. At the time, her role wasn't widely known. Today, Rosalind Franklin is celebrated as a pioneer and sometimes called "the dark lady of DNA."

Humans and chimpanzees share 98.8% of their DNA.

Ever wondered just how similar humans are to chimps? The answer is: very similar. In fact, human DNA and chimpanzee DNA are 98.8% the same!

Of course, that doesn't mean chimps will start behaving like humans anytime soon. That last 1.2% includes a whole lot of differences that added up over a whole lot of time. It's also important to note there can be big differences in how certain genes are expressed, even if the DNA overlaps. That said, we're still similar enough that chimpanzees can catch some diseases we usually think of as "human" illnesses, such as the flu or the common cold. The next time you go to the zoo, make sure you're healthy—because a chimpanzee's immune system can't fight those illnesses the way we humans can.

Fact or Fiction?

Your bones are strong enough to carry five pick-up trucks!

Fact!

It turns out Superman isn't the only "Man of Steel." We all are! Scientists have found that 1 cubic inch of human bone can hold the weight of five pickup trucks before breaking! It takes an incredible amount of force to even crack a thigh bone (or *femur*), let alone break it. Humans aren't indestructible, though. Even the strongest bones can break. Like most bones, your femur is still long and thin, which means it can still break if it's hit with enough force at just the right angle.

The more nutrition and exercise you give your body, the stronger your bones will be. On the other hand, if you treat your body poorly, your bones can become weaker and easier to break. It's a good reminder that even though our bodies are strong, unlike Superman, humans aren't invincible.

Your pinky finger is no slouch.

Your pinky finger might look small and weak, but it actually has an important job for your body. Scientists say that as much as one-third of your grip strength comes from your pinky finger! That means if you didn't have a pinky finger, you wouldn't be able to grip things nearly as hard. Think about that next time you make a pinky promise!

Ever wondered why it's called your "pinky" finger? "Pinky" actually comes from the Dutch word *pink*, which means "little finger." In English, people have been calling our smallest finger the pinky finger since the early 1800s!

Some people cough if you put something in their ear.

A small percentage of people have a condition called *Arnold's nerve reflex*, which causes them to cough when something (like a finger or a cotton swab) enters their ear. The condition isn't dangerous, but it can be embarrassing for some people. It can also be annoying; if earwax builds up in the ear, Arnold's nerve reflex can trigger coughing fits.

In severe cases, doctors can prescribe medication to make the nerve that causes the condition less sensitive. But this is only necessary if the problem has gotten pretty extreme.

Your heart will probably beat more than 2 billion times in your life.

The average person's heart beats roughly 100,000 times per day. That translates to around 35 million beats per year. That means that if you live into your 70s, your heart will beat more than 2.5 billion times!

Of course, not everyone's heart beats at the same rate. If you have a high heart rate, your number of beats will probably be higher. If you have a low heart rate, it will be lower. And if you live to be 80 or even 100 years old, you might hit 3 or 4 billion beats!

There are more bacteria cells in your body than "human" cells.

Your body isn't just made of up skin cells, blood cells, muscle cells, and other "human" cells. There are trillions of bacteria cells called *microbes* throughout the human body! Those little microbes help us do all kinds of things. Most of them exist in our guts, including the stomach and the intestines, where they perform important tasks like helping us break down and digest our food. When doctors talk about "gut flora" or "healthy bacteria," this is what they mean.

Scientists estimate that the average human body has roughly 30 trillion human cells and 39 trillion bacteria cells. It's pretty weird to know that we're outnumbered in our own bodies!

When you blush, your stomach blushes with you.

Almost everyone has blushed before. Some of us have even gotten caught blushing, which makes us blush even more. Have you ever wondered what *actually* happens when you blush? When you feel embarrassed, blood rushes to your face and turns your cheeks red. But your face isn't the only thing that turns red when you blush. Scientists have found that blood also rushes to your stomach lining, turning your stomach red along with your cheeks!

You might have Neanderthal DNA.

Neanderthals were a closely related human species that went extinct around 40,000 years ago. But before they did, Neanderthals and *Homo sapiens*, the species of humans we are, existed together. Even though Neanderthals haven't been around for thousands of years, we can still see evidence of them in our DNA. In fact, in most places on the planet, anywhere from 1 to 4% of your DNA may have come from Neanderthals.

Today, only one species of human, *Homo sapiens*, lives on our planet. But it's pretty cool to think that tens of thousands of years ago, we had distant cousins walking the Earth alongside us!

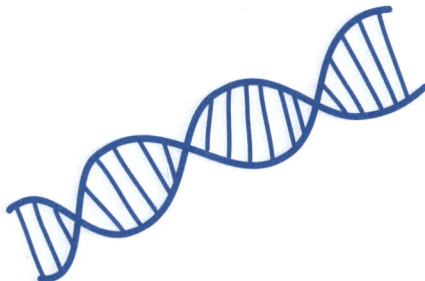

Humans are incredible long-distance runners.

The human body has evolved to be amazing at long-distance running. When it comes to sprinting, we may not be the fastest creatures in the animal kingdom, but we can catch up to just about anything. Scientists think this gave early humans an advantage when it came to hunting. We could track and chase down animals over long distances, wearing them down until they became too tired to keep going.

We can tell this is true for a few reasons. First, humans have an unusually high number of sweat glands, which allow us to sweat more and cool ourselves down. The fact that we stand upright and run on two legs also helps us use energy more efficiently than animals that need to power all four legs. We may not be as fast as a cheetah, but we're still pretty remarkable.

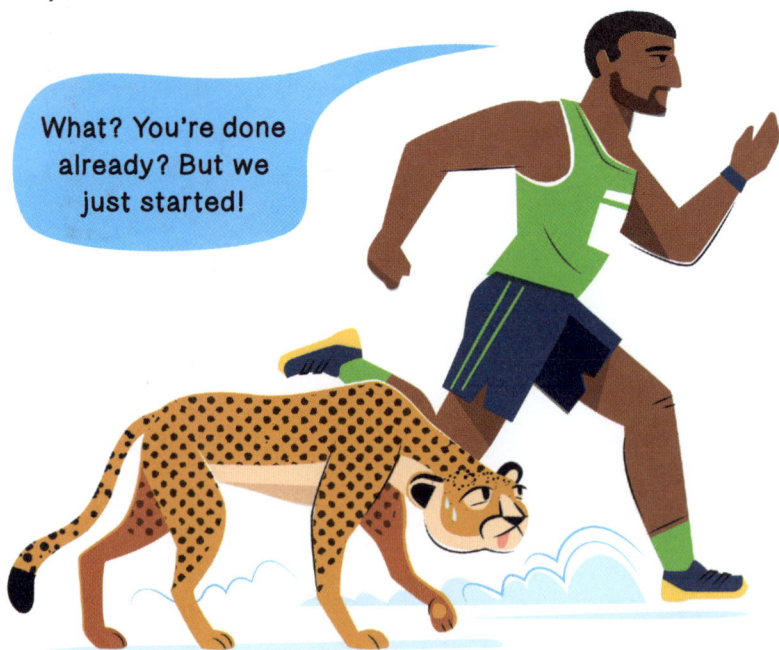

Your intestines are longer than you are tall.

And then some! You probably know that the human digestive system has both a small intestine and a large intestine. But did you know that together, your intestines can be more than 20 feet long? On average, the large intestine is about 5 feet long, while the small intestine can be anywhere from 10 to 34 feet long!

In order to fit inside your body, your intestines are coiled up below your stomach like a snake. They wind their way through your gut, digesting food and pushing it from your stomach toward, well . . . the toilet.

It's not rare for a person to have three kidneys instead of two.

When someone gets a kidney transplant, usually doctors don't bother taking the original kidney out (unless it is causing pain or creating health risks). Instead, they just hook the new one up and leave the old one behind!

It might sound weird, but it's actually safer this way. Removing an organ is serious business, and it can create a lot of risks. If the original kidney isn't causing any other problems (aside from, you know, not working properly), leaving it there is less risky than removing it.

Fact or Fiction?

You can be allergic to water.

It sounds impossible, but some people have a rare condition called aquagenic urticaria. When their skin touches water—yes, even clean, regular water—they break out in red, itchy rashes.

Fact!

This makes everyday activities like showering or swimming extremely difficult. Even sweat, rain, or tears can trigger a reaction. The rash usually appears within minutes and can last for hours.

While it's not technically an "allergy" in the strict scientific sense—because the immune system isn't reacting to a foreign invader—it acts like one. Scientists think the reaction may be caused by a combination of water and certain natural substances in the skin, or changes in skin temperature that confuse the body's immune response.

Fewer than 100 cases have been documented worldwide, which makes it one of the rarest skin conditions known. People with aquagenic urticaria often manage symptoms with antihistamines or barrier creams, but there's currently no cure.

So yes, water may be essential to life—but for a few unlucky people, it's also a serious problem.

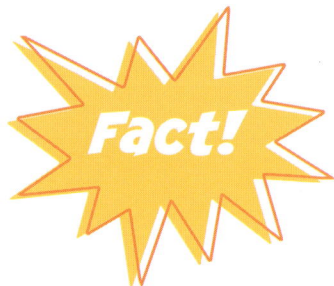

The world's loudest burp was louder than a jet engine.

The loudest burp ever recorded by a human hit 112.4 decibels—that's louder than a car horn, but not quite jet-engine loud.

Fiction!

To compare: a car horn is about 110 decibels, a chainsaw is around 120, and a jet engine during takeoff can hit 140 decibels or more. At that level, sounds can cause immediate hearing damage. So while the burp was booming, it didn't reach aircraft levels.

The record was set in 2021 by Neville Sharp from Australia, who trained for years to perfect his powerful belch. He beat the previous world record by over 4 decibels—a big jump in sound energy. Sound levels are measured on a logarithmic scale, which means each 10-decibel increase is about 10 times more intense to the human ear.

So Sharp's burp wasn't just loud—it was scientifically impressive. And yes, it was measured using professional sound equipment in a controlled environment to make it official. Loud, gross, and Guinness-approved.

When You Were Born . . .

You were color-blind.

That's right, all babies are color-blind. A newborn baby's eyes are still developing. They can tell the difference between black and white and recognize a few bright colors, but they don't have fully developed color vision until they are five months old.

It's more important for babies to be able to focus on objects and develop depth perception than to see in color, because those skills help them recognize things in the world around them (and avoid bumping into them). Color vision is nice, but it's less important to their development—which is why it comes later in the growing process.

You had more bones than your parents.

When babies are born, they usually have around 300 bones. But most adults have just 206 bones. What gives? Where do the extra bones go?

Actually, they don't go anywhere. A lot of those extra bones are made of cartilage, a material that's more flexible than normal bone. The extra cartilage helps keep babies from breaking bones while they're still vulnerable. As they grow older, those smaller, cartilage bones fuse together to form bigger, tougher bones. And that's how you wind up with 206 bones!

People with red hair need extra anesthesia during surgery.

For a long time, doctors reported that redheads needed extra anesthesia during medical procedures. When scientists finally got around to studying the problem, they found it was true! On average, people with naturally red hair need about 20% more anesthesia to get the same numbing effect as people with other hair colors. This is because redheads have a certain mutation that people with other hair colors usually don't have, and it can affect their pain receptors. That's why redheads are sometimes more sensitive to pain, too.

You can taste garlic with your feet.

Do you ever smell or taste garlic, even though you haven't gone anywhere near it? That's because garlic contains a molecule called *allicin* that can enter the skin of your feet and travel through your bloodstream to your mouth and nose. As strange as it sounds, you can taste (and smell!) garlic with your feet. It sounds unbelievable, but it's true! You can even try it for yourself: Put a few garlic cloves in your socks and wait an hour or so. Sooner or later, you'll swear you can smell garlic in the air!

Eating too many carrots can turn your skin orange.

You can never eat too many fruits and vegetables, right? Well, sort of. If you eat too many carrots, the pigment that gives carrots their orange color might turn *you* orange, too! As shocking as it would be to see your skin turn orange, it's actually harmless. And you'd have to eat around 10 carrots a day for a few weeks straight. But don't worry, it's also easy to reverse: Just stop eating so many carrots! In fact, doctors say babies are more likely to develop this condition. Since their diet is made up mostly of mushy carrots and other vegetables, babies can accidentally eat more carrots than the recommended quantity.

Myth Busters!

You only lose 10 to 15% of your heat through your head.

That's right. It's a complete myth that we lose a large majority (80%) of our heat through heads. We lose heat through our skin. The surface area of the top of your head is not that large and obviously isn't larger than the rest of your skin. This myth most likely comes from a 1970s US Army survival manual. The manual suggested that a person loses "40 to 45% of body heat" through their heads and should always cover their heads when it's cold. Now, when an adult tells you to wear your hat, you can explain to them that as long as you are dressed for the weather in other ways, you'll probably be okay without a hat.

Sugar doesn't actually make kids hyperactive.

You've probably heard it a thousand times: If you have too much sugar, you'll be bouncing off the walls! It's time to bust that myth. In fact, research has shown pretty clearly that there's no connection between sugar and hyperactive behavior. They have done experiments to study the effects of sugar on kids using a placebo (remember, that means "fake"). Guess what? Sugar was shown not to affect the kids' behavior. Could it be the placebo effect at work? Either way, the next time an adult tells you candy will make you hyper, you can say, "Actually, researchers have found no evidence to support that claim. One candy bar, please!"

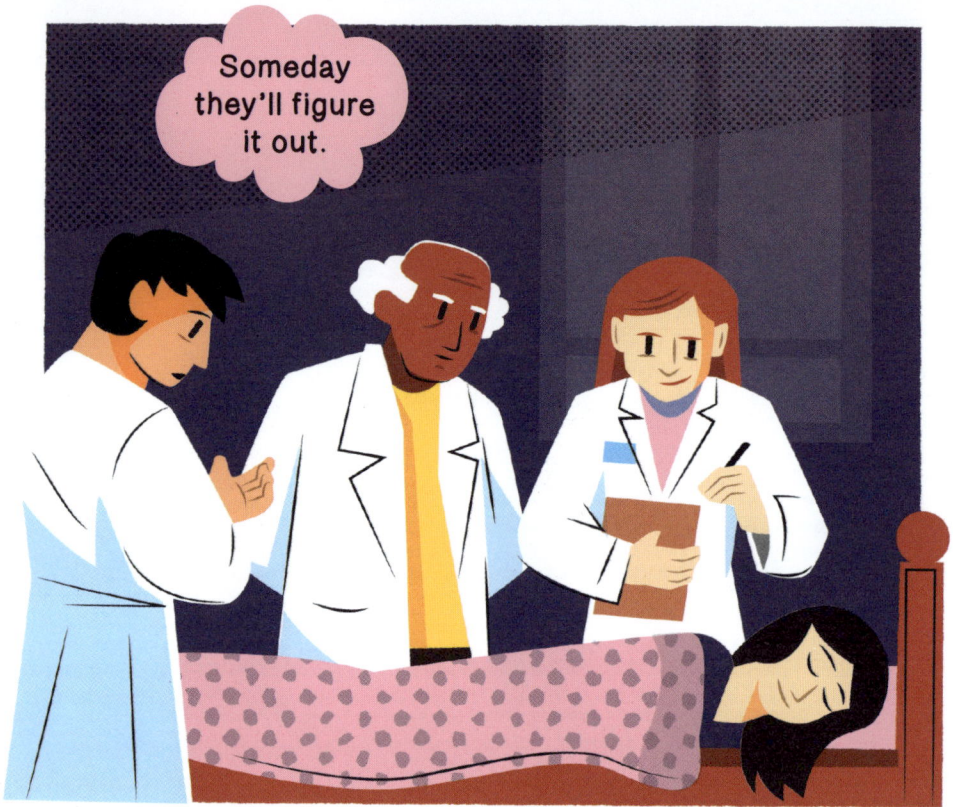

Scientists don't know why we need to sleep.

The average human spends about 8 hours a day sleeping, but different animals need different amounts of sleep. Elephants need just 2 hours of sleep. On the other hand, koalas can sleep up to 22 hours per day! But the fascinating thing about sleep is that scientists still aren't sure why we do it.

Some scientists think it's a way for the body to save energy, while others think it gives the body a chance to repair itself. Some say sleep helps our brains in ways we don't yet understand. Whatever the case, it sure feels nice to get a good night's sleep!

Fact or Fiction?

Your brain is still active while you sleep.

In fact, some parts of your brain are even *more* active while you sleep. The areas of your brain that focus on things like information processing and emotion are often more active when your body is asleep. Scientists believe these parts of the brain work together to sort and process everything that happened while you were awake, which helps you wake up refreshed and ready to face the next day.

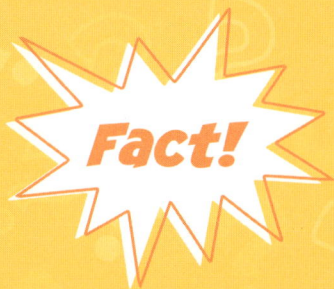

Fact!

There are a few different types of sleep. There is *light sleep* and *deep sleep*. There's also *REM sleep*, which is when you dream. "REM" stands for "rapid eye movement," and if you've ever watched someone have a bad dream, you know that's *exactly* what happens! When you dream, your eyes move around under your eyelids—almost like you're seeing the dream in real life. Scientists aren't sure why REM sleep is necessary, but we do know humans aren't the only animals that dream. Dogs, cats, rats, and even spiders all dream, too!

PLANTS & ANIMALS

Plants and animals have been around for a long time, and some have evolved in pretty unique ways. Some have grown large, some have grown small, and some can almost live forever! Some animals even have accents. Some plants look like animals, and some fruit (like bananas!) is radioactive. Did you know that technically, there is no such thing as a vegetable? (Just wait until your parents hear that!)

But . . . are cow farts really harmful to our climate? Can chickens see more colors than humans? Do snails have more teeth than sharks? Learn the answers to these questions and much more in this section, chock-full of mind-blowing facts like who discovered the famous theory of evolution "survival of the fittest"?

I bet you didn't know there's an animal that poops in cubes (seriously). Ready to find out which one?

Let's dive into the fantastic world of plants and animals!

Fact or Fiction?

Cow farts cause climate change.

Well, mostly.

Cows go through a digestive process called *enteric fermentation*, where sugars are broken down by other molecules. This process also produces methane gas. Methane is one of the most powerful (and smelly) greenhouse gases. Even though methane molecules don't last long in the air, each one can trap a lot of heat. That means methane is one of the major reasons for global warming.

Fact!

So while cows *do* fart methane gas, the majority of the methane is actually released through their burps—not their farts. Thankfully, methane is odorless!

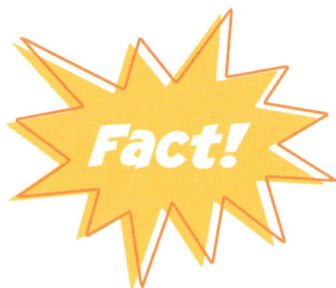

In nature, an "alpha wolf" isn't a real thing.

People use the term "alpha wolf" (or "alpha dog") to describe someone with a take-charge attitude. The leader of the pack. The person everyone else looks up to for tough decisions. It comes from the idea that wolf packs have one clear leader (or "alpha") that the rest of the group follows. Dogs, which are closely related to wolves, also have one clear leader who rises above the pack. At least, that's what most people think.

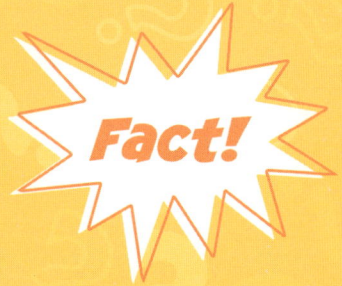

Fact!

Here's the *real* truth: While scientists have seen wolf packs fall in behind an "alpha," they have only seen it happen with wolves in captivity. Often, wolves in captivity are unrelated, and when they are forced to live together, a hierarchy forms. However, in nature wolves mostly live in family packs—a breeding pair and their offspring. Therefore, parents generally guide the activities of the pack. But this is different from displaying dominance. It turns out wolves only follow a dominant leader when they are held in a zoo, lab, or other unnatural place . . . like a movie theater!

Double Take

Double Take

There's an orchid that looks like a bird in flight.

At first glance, the moth orchid could be mistaken for a bird or a moth. It's true! If you look closely at the bloom of this orchid, you can make out a bird's head. The center of the orchid points down, kind of like a beak, and on either side of it are two reddish dots that look like eyes. The wall of petals that surround the "head" looks like wings spread out in flight. On top of this, the moth orchid is a mix of fuchsia and white, with a touch of yellow, making this plant not only cool but beautiful to look at. Go ahead and do a double-take.

Bees have a doppelganger in nature.

It's called a bee orchid, and its center literally looks like a bee. But nothing in nature is random. This bee lookalike is the orchid's clever way of attracting . . . you guessed it, bees! The center of this orchid mimics a female bee, including its scent and furry black-and-yellow appearance, offering male bees the false promise of love. This hoodwink draws in male bees so the flower can be pollinated. Sneaky, sneaky!

Crows are as smart as a 7-year-old human.

Other than humans, crows might be the smartest animals on Earth. Researchers say crows can solve problems, recognized faces, use tools, and even make plans for the future—which most animals *definitely* can't do. In fact, scientists say this makes crows about as smart as an average 7-year-old human!

Of course, even a 7-year-old is smarter than a crow in most ways. For instance, crows will never be able to have a conversation (or read a book like this one!).

If an alligator egg gets too hot, the baby will be male.

If the eggs get too cold, they only produce females. The sex of an alligator is decided by the temperature of the egg during its development—and scientists still aren't sure why!

The temperatures aren't all that different, either. If the eggs are kept below 86°F, they will produce 100% females. If the eggs are kept above 91.4°F, they will be 100% male. That's barely a 5° difference! Weird, right?

Fact or Fiction?

Bats are blind.

You've probably heard the phrase "blind as a bat," but that's actually not true. Bats aren't blind—in fact, most species have vision nearly as good as humans, and some fruit bats (called megabats) that fly during the day can see very well in bright sunlight.

Fiction!

But bats are famous for something even cooler: echolocation. This is a kind of biological sonar—like superhero hearing! Bats send out high-frequency sound waves—too high for human ears to hear—and then listen for the echoes that bounce off nearby objects. Their brains create a mental map of the world using only sound.

This amazing ability helps microbats hunt tiny flying insects in total darkness with incredible accuracy. So not only can bats see—they can "see" with sound too. Next time someone says, "blind as a bat," you'll know bats actually have two powerful ways to navigate—and they're both awesome.

The largest living thing on Earth is a mushroom.

It might sound like science fiction, but the biggest living thing on the planet isn't a whale or a redwood tree—it's a fungus!

Fact!

Deep underground in Oregon's Malheur National Forest, a single organism called the honey mushroom (*Armillaria ostoyae*) spreads across more than 2,300 acres—that's about 3.5 square miles (or 9 square kilometers) of forest floor. It's all connected by a massive network of underground threads called mycelium, which act like roots for fungi.

Scientists believe this giant fungus could be over 2,000 years old—and possibly even older.

While we mostly see mushrooms popping up above ground, those are just the "fruit." The real body of the fungus stays hidden below.

So yes, Earth's largest known organism is a humble mushroom.

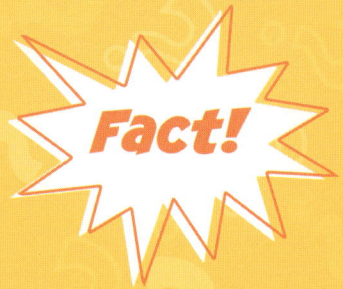

Animal Superpowers

Trout have a compass in their nose.

That doesn't just mean trout are good at knowing which way is north—it's literally true! Scientists have taken cells from a trout's nose and observed them under a microscope. They found that if they put a magnet nearby, those cells would point right to it!

Scientists have always wondered how animals seem to sense Earth's magnetic field. This discovery may have put them one step closer to solving that mystery.

Chickens can see colors humans can't.

Different animals see the world in different ways. Things like eye placement (some animals have their eyes on the side of their head, while others have eyes that face forward) and eye shape can change the way certain animals take in the sights. How well animals see color is determined by "cones" in the eyes that sense light and detect different colors. The human eye has three types of cones, which are capable of sensing red, green, and blue light. That means every color humans can see is made up of some combination of those three colors. Chickens, on the other hand, have *four* types of cones that can detect red, green, blue, and purple. That means chickens can see more color combinations and shades than we can!

Ants can lift 50 times their body weight.

The strongest animal on Earth isn't the elephant, or the rhinoceros, or any other large creature. It's the ant! Ants are all pretty strong, but some species of ant can lift up to 50 times their own bodyweight. That's the equivalent of a 150-pound human lifting 7,500 pounds—about the weight of a pickup truck!

Ants need to be strong because they spend most of their lives digging tunnels and foraging for food. The more dirt they can move or food they can bring back, the more valuable they are to the colony.

Dolphins can see in two directions at once.

Dolphins are amazing animals for many reasons, one of which is their extraordinary vision. Dolphins can see things above water and underwater due to their ability to auto-correct their eye shape. They also have special cells in their retina that allow them to see in both bright and dim light. But one of the coolest things about dolphins is that their eyes move independently of each other! That means they can look in front, to the side, and even partly behind themselves at the same time—now *that's* an amazing superpower!

Fact or Fiction?

All flowers smell good.

Sadly, this isn't true. In fact, the world's biggest flower is the *Rafflesia arnoldii*, which is also known as the "stinking corpse lily." You can probably guess what it smells like . . . rotting flesh. Yuck!

Fiction!

Despite their terrible smell, Rafflesia flowers are fascinating. They can grow to be an incredible 4 feet wide, with 5 massive petals around the center. The petals emit the rotten smell to attract flies for pollination. This flower is stinky *and* sneaky!

Gorillas are capable of speaking English at a first-grade level.

But they are capable of communicating at a toddler level! Primates are our closest relatives in the animal kingdom, and over time scientists have tried to teach gorillas and other monkeys to communicate. The most successful experiment involved teaching American Sign Language to a gorilla named Koko. Over the years, Koko learned to sign more than 1,000 words (roughly the vocabulary of a three-year-old child)!

Before Koko, the most famous animal language experiment involved a chimpanzee named Nim. Nim was raised by a human family, as if he were a human child. But the experiment ended in failure when he started to get too violent for his "parents" to manage.

Fiction!

HOW IT WORKS

How Did We Domesticate Animals?

One of the most impressive things humans have done is domesticate certain animals. Some, like dogs and cats, are considered pets. Others, like cows, pigs, and sheep, are considered livestock. No other animal on the planet has domesticated another species. So, how did we do it?

The answer is *selective breeding*. Certain traits make animals more desirable to humans, such as how friendly they are, how well they can be trained, and how comfortable they are in captivity. Humans looked for animals with those traits and brought them together to create similar offspring. Over a long, long period of time, humans turned dangerous animals like wolves into friendly dogs! Of course, humans weren't just looking for friends: Dogs are very helpful hunting partners, and domesticated cows and chickens can make tasty things like milk, eggs, and cheese. Sheep produce wool that is important for clothing, and horses help humans get around much more quickly.

Selective breeding is still something we do today, but it's usually not about survival. Humans have created different breeds of dogs with small bodies that make them easy to carry around or soft fur that doesn't make people with allergies get sick. We've also bred animals like chickens to increase their size, so each individual chicken produces more food. Domesticating animals is one of the most impressive ways humans have shaped the world to meet our needs.

Rats are ticklish.

Humans aren't the only creatures that can be tickled. Scientists have discovered that rats enjoy the feeling of being tickled, and even let out high pitched squeaks that sound like laughter! They definitely seem to enjoy it; some rats will jump for joy after being tickled, and they will often return to the spot where they were tickled in the hopes of being tickled again!

But rats aren't the only ticklish animals. Some primates (like chimpanzees and gorillas) can be tickled. That's not surprising since they're our closest animal relatives. Some dogs are also ticklish, and scientists think sharks might be, too! But most of those creatures don't laugh when they're tickled. That's a special reaction reserved for humans and rats, apparently!

Gross But True!

Lobsters pee through their eyes.

Weird as it sounds, lobsters urinate through a gland under their eyeballs. So if you see a lobster that looks like it's crying, those tears are probably something much more gross.

Urine actually plays an important role in how lobsters have babies. A female lobster's pee contains pheromones (a sort of "smell") that lets the male lobster know she is ready to mate. Male lobsters sometimes pee on each other as a way to fight and show dominance. Aren't you glad humans don't communicate that way?

There's a spider that looks like bird poop.

Everyone knows chameleons can change the color of their skin to blend in with their environment. But they're not the only creatures in the animal kingdom that have become very good at hiding themselves.

Meet the "Bird Dung Spider." Native to Australia and New Zealand, this little guy hides by making itself look like, well, bird poop! This creature's coloring is brown, black, and white, and it rests in place with its legs tucked underneath its triangle-shaped abdomen. This spider may not be pretty, but it is smart: After all, who wants to go near bird poop?

Wombats poop cubes.

Everybody poops, and that includes animals. But some animals have more interesting poop than others. Take the wombat, for example. This little marsupial is the only animal in the world that poops in the shape of a cube! Scientists aren't exactly sure why this happens, but they think it probably has something to do with the wombat's unusual digestive system and the shape of its gut. They aren't the only animals with strange poop, but they're definitely among the weirdest.

There is a species of turtle that can breathe through its butt.

Okay, technically these turtles don't breathe through their butts, but that's mostly just because turtles don't have butts. Like birds, they have a single opening called a *cloaca*, and, yes, the opening is in their behind. Sometimes tutles even use it to breathe underwater. It's not as effective as regular breathing, so turtles usually don't do it for very long. But some species of river turtles are so good at butt breathing (okay, fine, "cloacal respiration") that they can stay underwater for hours!

Hippos sweat sunscreen.

Hippos live in hot, dry environments, so you might wonder why they don't get sunburned. The answer is simple: They make their own sunscreen! Hippos naturally "sweat" a reddish substance that scatters sunlight and prevents the animal's skin from burning. Scientists have even studied hippo sweat to see if they could learn anything that would allow them to create more effective sunscreen for humans. This type of research is called *biomimicry*, and it helps us learn from other parts of the animal kingdom.

Fact or Fiction?

Bananas are radioactive.

Bananas contain a *slightly* radioactive form of potassium, which means bananas themselves are technically radioactive. Don't worry, though: The radiation level is incredibly small, which means you don't need to worry about getting too close to a banana. In fact, scientists say you'd have to eat around 10 million bananas (all in one sitting!) before radiation poisoning would set in. So no matter how much you like bananas you don't need to worry.

Bananas aren't the only food that is technically radioactive. Potatoes, sunflower seeds, and many types of nuts all contain potassium, too. But, like bananas, the amount is far too small for humans to worry about. So, go bananas!

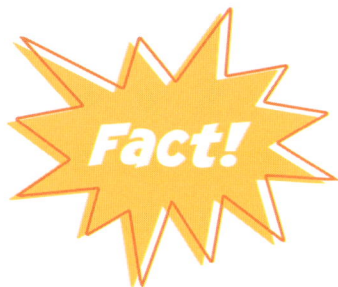

Fact!

Sharks have been around longer than trees.

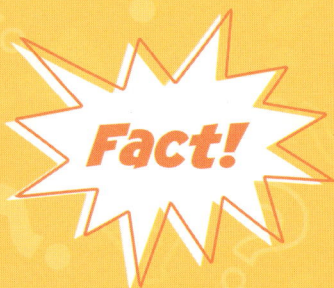

The earliest shark fossils date back at least 450 million years, to the Ordovician Period. Trees didn't evolve on Earth until about 390 million years ago, and dinosaurs appeared approximately 250 million years ago. That means when the first sharks began swimming in the ocean, there wasn't a single tree anywhere on the planet. The climate during this period was warmer and more tropical than it is now, and the animals and plants lived mostly in the water.

Sharks aren't the only creatures that have been around longer than you might expect. There are also species of jellyfish that scientists believe date back more than 500 million years—and sea sponges that may have been around 700 million years ago!

Fact!

Charles Darwin: The Father of Evolution

Charles Darwin's theory of natural selection helped explain how evolution works. It says organisms that change or evolve traits to better adapt to their environment are more likely to survive and reproduce, passing those traits down. From 1831 to 1836, Darwin boarded the HMS *Beagle* and traveled from England to Australia, stopping in Africa, South America, and the Indian Ocean islands. He studied plants and animals in each location and saw how they changed to match their environment. This gave us a new understanding of evolution. His book, *On the Origin of Species*, was based on this research.

One thing you might not know: Darwin didn't just discover animals—he ate them! He was known for trying exotic creatures and documenting his dining adventures. Armadillos, pumas, ostriches, iguanas, and even giant tortoises were among his meals. Given his time aboard the *Beagle*, Darwin may have eaten more animals than anyone in history!

Giraffes have black tongues so their tongues don't get sunburned.

Since giraffes are so tall, they don't spend a lot of time in the shade. In fact, they spend most of their time eating leaves from the tops of trees, which means sunburns can be a real problem. In fact, scientists think that giraffes may have developed their unique black tongues specifically to avoid this problem! They say the giraffe's black tongue works like natural sunscreen, helping to protect it from the sun's harmful rays. That means giraffes can spend as much time as they want slurping down delicious leaves without having to worry about a nasty sunburn.

Goats have accents.

Not all goats sound the same! As goats get older and learn to "speak," their voices naturally start to sound more like the other goats around them. That means if you take two goats from different parts of the country, their voices will have different "accents"!

Goats and humans aren't the only species that can develop accents based on their surroundings. Elephants and dolphins also change the way they sound depending on their social environment. In fact, dolphins have unique accents according to where they live in the world—just like goats and humans!

Today's birds come from dinosaurs.

While the dinosaurs went extinct following an asteroid impact about 66 million years ago, they didn't all die. Some smaller dinosaurs survived and changed to meet their new conditions. These dinosaurs were known as theropods, and they evolved into what we now know as birds. Over time, they lost their teeth and evolved beaks, and their arms gradually turned into wings.

Sadly, not every theropod was able to make the evolutionary leap. The T-Rex is also from the theropod family, but only smaller species were able to survive long enough to evolve into birds. That's too bad—can you imagine flocks of T-Rexes flying around today?

Dinosaurs were around for a long, long time.

Humans have only been around for about 200,000 years. Compare that to the dinosaurs, who roamed Earth for an astonishing 165 million years! That's a long, long time, and not all dinosaurs existed at the same time. For example, the Stegosaurus lived about 150 million years ago, while the T-Rex evolved pretty late—only about 67 million years ago. That means less time separates humans and the T-Rex than the T-Rex and the Stegosaurus!

Even though the T-Rex is one of the most popular dinosaurs, it wasn't around for very long. The meteor that wiped out the dinosaurs arrived 66 million years ago, so the T-Rex only had 1 million years or so to terrorize its fellow dinos.

Fact or Fiction?

Red food coloring is made from bugs.

Red food coloring is often made from cochineal extract, which comes from the dried bodies of cochineal insects. The bugs are dried in the sun, soaked in alcohol, and processed to create a bright red color.

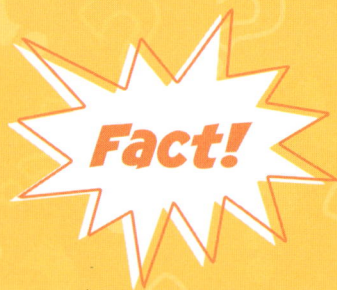

Fact!

Don't worry, it's perfectly safe (well, unless you are allergic to cochineal!). And you might be surprised just how many foods include this coloring. But some people just don't like the idea of bugs in their food. The nerve!

It could be worse, though. Throughout history, humans have used a lot of gross (and unhealthy) things to change the color of food. Harmful ingredients like arsenic, mercury, and even lead have been used as food dye. So, bugs beat poison any day!

Birds eat rocks to help them digest their food.

Birds don't have teeth, which means they can't grind their food the way humans and other animals do. They need a little extra help—and they get it from rocks. Birds will often eat tiny pieces of rock (called grit), which helps them break down hard-to-digest foods. This is necessary to make sure birds actually get the nutrients they need from what they eat. Otherwise those nutrients would pass right through them! So if you ever see birds outside pecking at pebbles, don't worry. Those rocks serve a purpose.

You could swim in a blue whale's veins (but you definitely shouldn't).

The blue whale is the largest animal on Earth, and *every* part of it is big. For example, a blue whale's heart is the size of a small car, and its tongue weighs as much as an elephant! Most impressive of all, a blue whale's blood vessels are so large that a human being could swim through some of them. Of course, that would probably be a bad idea—not to mention an icky one.

Pumping blood through a blue whale's body is no easy task. That giant heart beats just once every 10 seconds, but it's loud enough to be heard from miles away!

Myth Busters!

Peanuts aren't actually nuts.

Even though the word "nut" is in the name, peanuts are not nuts. They are technically *legumes*, which means they are a member of the pea family! This sort of makes sense, right? The peanut shell isn't so different from a pea pod, after all. According to scientists, peanuts, soybeans, and lentils are all examples of edible seeds—not nuts.

Actually, a lot of "nuts" aren't really nuts. Cashews are seeds that grow from the bottom of a "cashew apple." Almonds, pistachios, and walnuts are seeds, too. Come to think of it, most of the things we consider nuts technically *aren't* nuts. But who cares? They're still delicious!

Plants aren't alive.

Trees and plants are living things, even if you can't see them move or hear them speak. What's more, some plants actually exhibit behaviors that suggest they react to stimuli like light, water, gravity, and touch happening around them. But while most trees are huge, living cells only make up a small fraction of their bulk. In fact, only 1% of a tree is actually alive and performing vital functions. The other, non-living cells aren't dead as much as they are dormant.

Still, if you're ever in a forest, keep your eyes peeled and your secrets to yourself. You never know. . . .

Scientists thought the platypus was a practical joke.

When the first platypus specimens were sent to Europe by Australian settlers, scientists thought someone was playing a prank on them. It's understandable: The platypus is one of the most unusual creatures in the world. It is the only mammal with a duck-like bill, and one of only five mammals that lay eggs. Throw in the fact that they have a beaver-like tail and venomous spikes on their hind legs, and you can see why scientists had a hard time believing they were real!

One scientist even poked around looking for stitches or other evidence that the platypus had been sewn together from other creatures!

A squid brain looks like a donut.

One of the squid's most unusual features is its brain. While most brains are a single, lumpy mass, the squid has a donut-shaped brain. Even stranger, the squid's throat passes through the center of the "donut." That means a squid could accidentally give itself brain damage if it tries to eat something too large! So even the biggest squid need to take tiny bites when they eat. Let that be a lesson to chew your food carefully!

An octopus has three hearts.

Octopuses are fascinating. They're incredibly smart creatures known to escape from their aquarium habitats. Their three hearts work together to oxygenate their large body and eight tentacles. They have one large heart that circulates blood from the gills to the rest of the body and two smaller hearts that pump blood to the gills. They also have blue blood and ink they can squirt in self-defense! Some octopuses can even change color like a chameleon.

Before you ask, yes, the plural of *octopus* can also be "octopi." But did you know there is a third option? Some linguists think *octopus* may have originally been a Greek word, which means the plural should be "octopodes." All three are used, but "octopuses" is most common today.

Fact or Fiction?

There is no such thing as a vegetable.

Fact!

Well, sort of. "Vegetable" is just a cooking term. Unlike fruit, vegetable is not an actual category of plants. According to *botanists* (aka plant scientists), the "fruit" is the part of the plant that contains the seeds. Strawberries, blueberries, and bananas are considered fruits. But you know what else are? Tomatoes, cucumbers, and peppers—even though we usually consider them vegetables. If you've ever heard someone tell you that a tomato is technically a fruit, now you know why!

Most of the things we consider vegetables are the roots, stems, and leaves of different plants. For instance, a carrot is a root. Asparagus is a stalk. Broccoli is a flower. Spinach is a leaf. But the next time your parents tell you to eat your vegetables, you can let them know that, technically, there's no such thing!

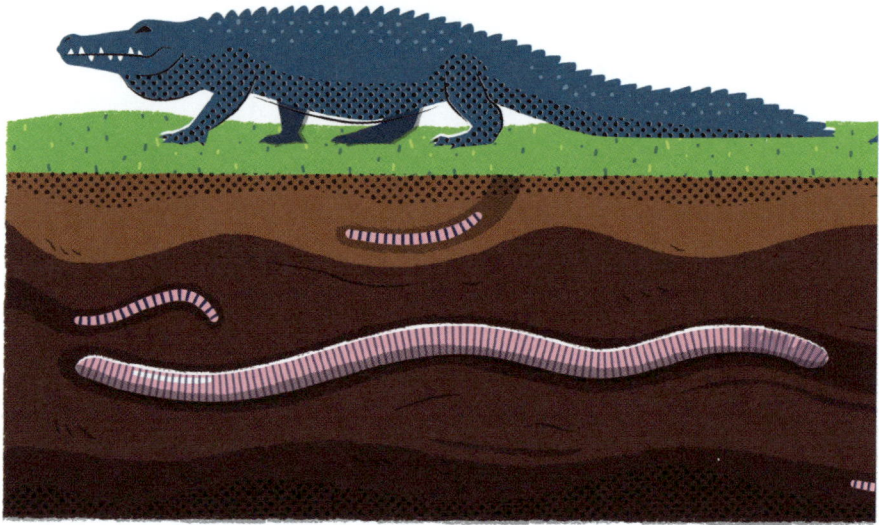

The largest worm in the world is almost 10 feet long!

The Giant Gippsland Earthworm is the largest worm ever discovered—and some of them can grow to be almost 10 feet long! Visually, the Giant Gippsland Earthworm doesn't look all that different from your standard earthworm aside from its shocking length. Like other earthworms, they move slowly underground, breaking down organic matter and improving the quality of the soil.

Unfortunately, being large isn't always an advantage. The Giant Gippsland Earthworm is considered a threatened species. They live in small, isolated colonies and mature very slowly compared to other worms. Luckily, Australian authorities have put a plan in place to help protect the long-term survival of the species.

Rabbits can't throw up.

Rabbits have a valve between their throat and their stomach that only opens one way. That means that once a rabbit has eaten something, it's not coming back (well, not *that* way, anyway). No matter how sick a rabbit is feeling, it will never throw up. It's physically impossible!

This might seem like a good thing—after all, nobody likes to vomit! But sadly, not having that ability can cause problems. Since rabbits can't throw up like dogs or cats, it can be harder to tell when a rabbit is sick. It's also harder for rabbits to clear blockages in their digestive system, which can cause some health problems. As gross as it can be to throw up, it actually serves a pretty important purpose!

Insects don't have lungs.

Animals need oxygen to survive—that's why we breathe, after all. But we don't get oxygen the same way. Everyone knows fish have gills, but did you know bugs breathe using a network of tubes called *tracheae*? It's true! Because of this, bugs don't breathe through their mouths the way most other animals do. Instead, oxygen enters through small openings called *spiracles*, where oxygen reaches the tracheae and is sent all over the insect's body. Pretty cool, right? Bugs can even close their spiracles when they want to, which is how bugs can basically hold their breath!

Fact or Fiction?

Moths can get as big as a pizza slice.

The Atlas moth (*Attacus atlas*) is one of the largest moths in the world, with a wingspan that can reach up to 10 inches—about the size of a large pizza slice and wider than most human hands! These gentle giants are found in Southeast Asia and are truly one of nature's wonders.

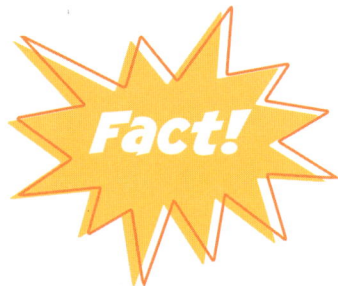

Fact!

Here's the wildest part: Atlas moth wings have markings that look just like snake heads. When a predator like a bird gets too close, the moth flashes its wings and shakes them, mimicking two angry cobras. This defense trick is called mimicry, and it's a clever way to scare off enemies—like having a built-in Halloween costume!

Even more surprising? Adult Atlas moths only live for one to two weeks. They don't have mouths and can't eat at all. Instead, they survive on the energy they stored as caterpillars—just long enough to find a mate and lay eggs.

Only humans go to war.

You might think that only humans fight organized wars, but our closest animal relatives—chimpanzees—have been caught doing the same thing!

The most famous example is the Gombe Chimpanzee War, which took place in Gombe National Park in Tanzania from 1974 to 1978. It was closely observed by the scientist Jane Goodall. What started as one big chimpanzee group split into two rival factions that became enemies.

Fiction!

For four whole years, these chimps fought like armies. They planned coordinated attacks and worked together to hunt down their former group members. It wasn't just random fighting—it was organized warfare that shocked scientists because it looked so much like human conflict.

By the end, one group had defeated the other and taken over their territory. Jane Goodall was so disturbed by the violence that she had nightmares about it.

So next time someone says only humans wage war, you can tell them that chimpanzees can be just as strategic and fierce.

Snails have more than 10,000 teeth.

Teeth are fascinating. Isn't it strange that our mouths are filled with little bones sticking out of our gums? Most adult humans have 32 teeth. That might sound like a lot, but compared to some of the other animals on Earth, it's practically nothing.

For example, crocodiles have 80 teeth. The great white shark has 300, while the whale shark has up to 3,000! In fact, sharks lose and regrow their teeth so often, they can have as many as 50,000 teeth over the course of their lives.

But the weirdest teeth in the animal kingdom don't belong to sharks or crocodiles. They belong to snails and slugs! The average garden snail has more than 10,000 teeth, and the rainbow slug has over 700,000! Don't let their tiny mouths fool you: These small creatures can chow down with the best of them.

Animals can be allergic to humans.

Lots of humans are allergic to animals like dogs or cats, but did you know it also works the other way around? Animals can be allergic to humans the same way humans are allergic to them! Animals with a human allergy might have itchy eyes, dry skin, runny noses, or sneezing fits. In other words, they act just like humans with an animal allergy.

Now that vets know animals can be allergic to humans, they are getting better at treating it. So don't worry—if your dog sneezes a lot around you, your vet can probably help!

Put me down! I said put me down!

This armadillo does *not* want to be picked up!

Did you know there is an armadillo nicknamed the "screaming hairy armadillo"? How did it earn that name, you ask? The answer is that whenever a human tries to pick one up, it has a habit of, well, *screaming*. The screaming hairy armadillo is found primarily in South America and is distinct from other armadillos, thanks to the long, bristly hairs that cover its armored body. Unfortunately for the armadillo, those hairs make it appear cuddlier than its hairless cousins . . . which is exactly why people want to pick it up!

Interestingly, the screaming hairy armadillo has an unusual diet. Like other armadillos, it's an omnivore, an animal that eats both plants and meat. But due to the dry, desert environment in which it lives, sand can be a problem. In fact, scientists estimate that at any given time, 50% of the screaming hairy armadillo's stomach may be filled with sand!

EARTH SCIENCE

Earth is a pretty incredible place. Features like the Grand Canyon and Mount Everest remind us just how beautiful and amazing this planet is, while hurricanes, tornadoes, and tsunamis remind us that it can also be unpredictable and even dangerous.

Have you ever wondered what the highest and lowest points on Earth are, where gold really comes from, or how to predict when it will rain? Get ready for some eye-opening facts. This section is filled to the brim with interesting facts about the world around you, the ground beneath your feet, and the sky above you. Did you know that the North Pole actually moves, so your compass needle won't always point to the same spot? Or that you could walk the distance of the world's smallest desert?

Get ready to learn who the "father of geology" is and how our Earth works.

Let's dig in!

Fact or Fiction?

Lightning is hotter than the surface of the sun.

Sort of. Since lightning bolts don't have a physical form, they don't have a temperature the way solid objects do. But we can measure how much lightning heats the air, and the answer is: a lot! When lightning strikes, the air it passes

Fact!

through is heated to around 50,000°F. That's roughly five times hotter than the surface of the sun! Thankfully, lightning strikes only last a fraction of a second, which means that heat *dissipates* (goes away) very quickly. When the air heats up, it expands, and when it cools down, it contracts. When that happens quickly, we hear a loud *boom*, and that's what we call thunder!

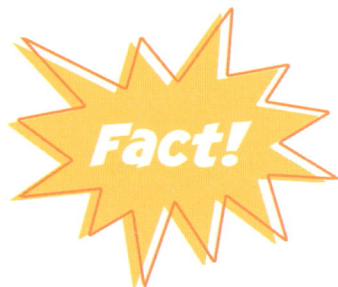

Thunder can also help you figure out how far away a storm is. When you see a lightning bolt, start counting until you hear the thunder. For every 5 seconds, it means the lightning strike was 1 mile further away. So if you count to 15 seconds before you hear the thunder, it means the storm is still 3 miles from you!

Women are four times more likely to be struck by lightning than men.

It's actually the exact opposite: Men are struck by lightning four times as often as women. Of course, this isn't because men naturally attract electricity. It's mostly because men tend to spend more time outside than women. Studies show men are more likely to have outdoor jobs than women— for example, men make up roughly 90% of construction workers and 70% of farm workers. Basically, that means men are just more likely to be outside during a thunderstorm. Research also shows that men are also more likely to take risks than women, so they wind up in more dangerous situations.

Fiction!

You've probably heard the saying "Lightning doesn't strike twice." Sadly, this isn't true. There are lightning "hotspots" scattered all over the Earth. In South America, Lake Maracaibo experiences roughly 233 lightning strikes per year, making it the most-struck location in the world.

Lightning strikes may be scary, but they usually aren't deadly: About 90% of people struck by lightning survive. But that doesn't mean you should avoid taking shelter in a storm. At least you'll keep your clothes dry inside!

Rain has a smell. Can your nose predict when it's coming?

Have you ever noticed that you can sometimes smell a rainstorm coming? That smell actually has a name: *petrichor*. People usually describe it an "earthy" scent, and it's produced when rain falls on dry soil. If it's been a while since the last rainstorm, it will probably smell particularly strong! Rainwater, ozone, plant oils, and a chemical compound called *geosmin* all contribute to the smell of petrichor. Geosmin is the main cause of the "earthy" smell; our noses are very sensitive to geosmin and can detect even tiny amounts in the air. Next time the weather says it's going to rain, go outside a few hours before and try to smell it coming!

How fast can you walk across the tiniest desert? Try it and see!

When you think of a "desert," you might picture endless sand dunes. But not all deserts are vast—some are surprisingly small. The world's smallest desert, the Carcross Desert in northern Canada, covers just 1 square mile. You could walk across it in only 15 minutes! The Carcross Desert was formed during the last glacial period. As glaciers melted, lakes formed. When the lakes dried up, the wind shaped the remaining sand into dunes. The Carcross Desert is home to rare plant species not typically found in northern Canada. Its unique environment makes it an interesting place for scientists and nature lovers alike. So, if you ever find yourself in the Yukon, consider a visit. It might be the quickest desert hike you'll ever take!

How many snowballs could you make from one giant snowflake?

Snowflakes can be huge.

You probably think of snowflakes as tiny little white specks falling from the sky. But that's not always the case—in fact, the biggest snowflake ever recorded was more than a foot wide! The giant snowflake was discovered outside Missoula, Montana, and measured an astonishing 15 inches wide and 8 inches thick. Some scientists are skeptical about whether a snowflake can really be that big, but the record stands for now.

Fact or Fiction?

Earth has two north poles.

When people talk about "the North Pole," they usually mean the geographic North Pole. That's the spot at the top of the world where all of the lines of longitude come together, and it is usually called the *true* North Pole.

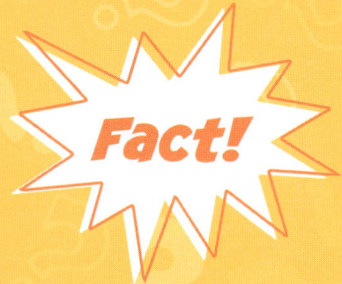

Fact!

The other north pole is the "magnetic North Pole." In scientific terms, this is the place where the Earth's magnetic field points directly downward, but most people just think of it as the spot where a compass needle points. Unlike the geographic North Pole, the magnetic North Pole doesn't stay in one place: It moves over time as the Earth's magnetic field changes. Don't worry, though. It always stays close to the geographic North Pole, so you can still rely on your compass to get home . . . at least for now (or until you get to the next page)!

Earth could have a giant, underground ocean.

Scientists believe Earth might have a massive underground ocean hidden deep within the planet's mantle. This ocean is located about 400 miles under the surface, and scientists say it could contain three times the water of Earth's surface oceans combined! They say it could help explain where the water on Earth's surface comes from.

Of course, this underground ocean doesn't look exactly like a normal ocean. Instead of being liquid, the water is trapped in a mineral called *ringwoodite*, which forms at very high temperatures. Scientists say the water contained in the ringwoodite may help keep our surface oceans stable and play an important part in the water cycle.

The Earth's magnetic poles sometimes flip-flop.

Every so often, the Earth's magnetic poles reverse. That means the North Pole becomes the South Pole, and the South Pole becomes the North Pole— kind of like Opposite Day. Your compass, which always points north, would start pointing toward Antarctica!

No one is exactly sure why the poles reverse, and it seems to happen at random. Over the past 160 million years, scientists think the poles have reversed a few hundred times. That's an average of once every 300,000 years or so. However, scientists say it hasn't happened for 780,000 years. Maybe we're due for a swap? If we are, don't worry too much. Things aren't going to change overnight. Even if the poles started reversing right now, it would take hundreds (maybe even thousands!) of years for the change to be complete.

HOW IT WORKS

Understanding Hurricanes

A hurricane is one of the most powerful and dangerous weather events on Earth, but how do they form? The answer is pretty cool!

When warm ocean water starts to evaporate, large clouds form and stretch high into the air. As this pattern continues, the clouds start moving in a circle around a point in the center. Eventually, this can become a large cluster of thunderstorms, which meteorologists call a tropical disturbance. As the storm gets bigger, it becomes unstable. Winds whip out from the middle of the storm as the air pressure changes. This causes even more thunderclouds to form, making the storm even bigger. Eventually, it becomes what scientists call a tropical depression.

At this point, it's just a question of how big the storm will get. Once the wind speeds inside the storm reach 39 miles per hour (mph), the tropical depression officially becomes a *tropical storm*. When the wind reaches 74 mph, the storm is officially a *hurricane*. A typical hurricane has clouds approximately 50,000 feet high and is roughly 125 miles across—but really big hurricanes can be larger than that!

Once a hurricane hits land, it usually gets weaker pretty quickly because it no longer has access to the warm ocean water that was making the storm so strong. Despite this, hurricanes still do a lot of damage on land.

A *Brocken specter* is a ghostly figure in the fog.

Foggy weather can create all kinds of strange optical illusions. Sometimes, when fog is really thick, your own shadow can be reflected and blown up, making it look like a giant ghostly figure is looming over you! These foggy ghosts are called *Brocken specters,* and they can be spooky. As you can probably imagine, they are the inspiration for many ghost stories and supernatural myths.

Brocken specters take their name from Brocken, a German mountain known for its foggy weather. The Brocken specter comes up a lot in local stories and folklore, but the phenomenon has been observed all over the world.

Fact or Fiction?

Scientists occasionally must add a *leap second* to the clock.

The Earth doesn't travel around the sun in exactly 365 days. It's more like 365 days . . . and 6 hours. Every 4 years, that adds up to an extra 24 hours, and we get a *leap year*.

Fact!

Leap seconds work the same way, but they're much smaller. Earth's rotation isn't exact—it can speed up or slow down for a few reasons, like changes in its core, earthquakes or volcanic eruptions, melting ice caps, and others. Those events are small, but they can add up. Every now and then, scientists agree to add 1 second to Earth's standard time.

If you're confused, don't worry: The process of adding leap seconds is going away. Computer systems can malfunction if different devices display different times—even if the difference is only one second. Since computers run practically everything these days, that means leap seconds are more trouble than they're worth.

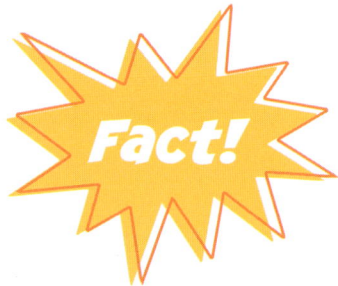

A *gravity hill* makes water run uphill.

Gravity hills are an optical illusion. Sometimes, the landscape around a hill can trick your brain into thinking you're going uphill when you're actually going downhill.

Fiction!

So to you it might look like water is running uphill, or a ball is rolling uphill, but in reality gravity is working the same way it always does!

As you can imagine, gravity hills (which are also called *magnetic hills*, *mystery hills*, and other names) have inspired lots of superstitions over the years. Before scientists understood how the illusion worked, many people believed supernatural forces were at play. Some have suggested magic, aliens, ghosts, or other supernatural things could be involved!

Get Ready, Rock Hunters!

Pyrite can form as a perfect cube.

You may have heard the phrase, "There are no straight lines in nature." That's usually true, but there are some exceptions. Take pyrite, for example. Pyrite (sometimes known as *fool's gold*) has a unique, cubic structure—and if it forms under the right conditions, it can create a perfect cube with pointed edges and straight sides. That's something you don't expect to see in nature!

One kind of rock can float on water.

Pumice is a type of rock formed during volcanic eruptions. When lava cools quickly, air bubbles can become trapped inside the rock as it solidifies, creating air pockets. The resulting rock is relatively light and not very dense—and if you put it in water, it will float to the top!

People use pumice in many ways, including cleaning and personal care. Pumice stones are used to remove dead skin or to help prevent or treat acne. The way pumice floats is neat, but the rough, harsh texture of the stone also makes it useful.

Rubies and sapphires are the same stone.

While rubies and sapphires are both precious gemstones, they are actually different types of the same mineral: corundum. Each stone gets its unique color from the different trace elements introduced during formation. Rubies get their red color from chromium, while sapphires turn blue from iron and titanium. Pretty cool, huh?

Chalk is mostly made from plankton skeletons.

When you look at chalk under a microscope, you might be surprised at what you find. This flaky form of limestone is formed from the remains of single-celled plankton, which get crushed into rock over millions of years. While some organic matter is turned into oil and other fossil fuels, these plankton formed the chalk you use to draw on the sidewalk! Probably not what you would've guessed, huh?

Some rocks produce sparks when smashed.

That's right! And when a rock gets smashed, not only does it spark—it also smells like fire! Quartz, milky quartz, and amethyst are a few rocks with a high amount of the compound called *silica*, which can create this lightning-like effect. This phenomenon is created by the friction that occurs when the rock is struck, and the smell of fire *is* actually the beginnings of a fire. That's why these rocks make great fire-starters in the woods. The next time you go camping, don't forget your rocks!

Fact or Fiction?

It once rained for more than a million years straight.

About 232 million years ago, an event called the *Carnian Pluvial* caused a massive change in Earth's climate. Up until that point, Earth had been mostly dry, but the Carnian Pluvial Event triggered a massive, planet-wide rainstorm that lasted 1 to 2 million years and continued pretty much nonstop.

Fact!

Most scientists believe the cause of this event was a bunch of volcanic eruptions that threw massive amounts of carbon dioxide into the air, which made the planet suddenly warm up. This rapid heating made it easy for huge monsoons to form and turned the dry planet into a wet one quickly. This event happened around the same time dinosaurs started walking the Earth. With more water available across the entire planet, it was much easier for life to survive!

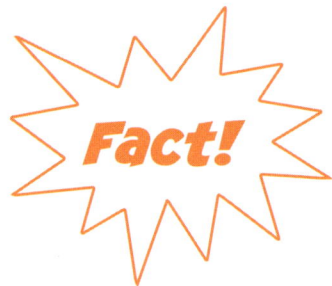

There are no volcanos in the Pacific Ocean.

Actually, about 75% of all volcanos on Earth are located in the "Ring of Fire" that surrounds the Pacific Ocean, and 90% of the world's earthquakes take place here, too! Over the past 12,000 years, 20 of the 25 biggest volcanic eruptions on Earth have all taken place within the Ring of Fire—including the 4 largest.

Fiction!

The Ring of Fire isn't actually a "ring." It's a horse-shoe-shaped formation formed by plate tectonics. And how do plate tectonics work? When two of the plates that form the Earth's crust collide, one is forced under the other. This pushes up lava, and the result is a volcano. The "ring" starts in northern New Zealand, travels up the coast of China, Japan, and Russia, makes the leap to Alaska. Finally, it winds down the western coast of North and South America all the way to the southern tip of Chile.

James Hutton Showed Us How the Earth Works

The "father of modern geology" was a man named James Hutton. Hutton lived from 1726 to 1797, at a time when most people thought Earth was only about 6,000 years old. He was a naturalist who was known for the way he examined the world around him, and his careful study of rocks and stones led him to a different belief. Hutton believed the Earth goes through a never-ending process of making and remaking. He thought pressure and heat played an important role in the formation of new rocks, and that volcanoes brought new materials to the surface to replace the land worn away by erosion. Hutton was basically right, and today his theories are still mostly accepted.

Hutton's work inspired countless other scientists. Sir Charles Lyell and Mary Horner Lyell, a pair of married geologists, built on Hutton's work to form their own theories. And the famous Charles Darwin (remember that guy?) said Hutton helped him understand that big changes can happen over a huge amount of time.

5 million years ago, the Mediterranean Sea dried up.

A few million years ago, the Mediterranean Sea was cut off from the Atlantic Ocean, causing the *Messinian Salinity Crisis*. Without the ocean to replenish it, the sea began to evaporate. Over the course of a few thousand years, nearly the entire Mediterranean Sea dried up, leaving behind a huge, salty basin roughly as deep as the Grand Canyon!

Eventually, tectonic shifts reconnected the Atlantic Ocean to the Mediterranean Basin, and water was able to come rushing in once more. Thankfully, this was long before humans were around because it was one heck of a flood!

Yellowstone National Park sits on top of a *supervolcano.*

Yellowstone National Park is famous for its hot springs and geysers—including the famous Old Faithful geyser. Yellowstone sits on top of an underground supervolcano that last erupted around 640,000 years ago. The heat from the magma chambers under Yellowstone is what creates the incredible attractions you can see when you visit the park.

The word "supervolcano" sounds scary, but don't worry: Scientists say there is very little chance the supervolcano under Yellowstone will erupt anytime in the next few thousand years. Scientists have gotten very good at guessing when volcanoes are going to erupt, which means we'll have plenty of notice if the Yellowstone supervolcano ever starts rumbling!

Raindrops fall between 15 to 25 miles per hour (mph).

Even though they're falling from high in the sky, rain-drops fall pretty slowly. At most, they can reach speeds of about 15 to 25 mph, depending on the size of the raindrop. This is because even the biggest raindrops are pretty small and don't have much mass. This small mass makes it easy for the air in Earth's atmosphere to create drag, which that slows them down. As a result, it doesn't matter how high up a raindrop falls; it will never go faster than 25 mph or so. This maximum falling speed is what scientists call terminal velocity.

Clouds are really heavy.

Clouds look fluffy and light. But actually, clouds are made up of huge amounts of water vapor, and even evaporated water can be heavy. Scientists say the aver-age cloud weighs more than a million pounds. That's as heavy as three blue whales combined!

So why do clouds float? They form when the sun causes water to evaporate, and that warm, wet air rises high into the sky. When the warm air hits cold air, it con-denses back into water vapor to form a cloud. As more warm air rises, it pushes the cloud upward, keeping the cloud in the sky—no matter how heavy it is!

There are seashell fossils on top of Mount Everest.

Mount Everest is the highest mountain in the world. So how have scientists and explorers found the remains of undersea creatures at its summit? The answer tells us a lot about how mountains form: 470 million years ago, the limestone formations that make up the top of Mount Everest formed at the bottom of the ocean. Over time, Earth's shifting tectonic plates pushed those formations higher and higher until they became the highest point in the world! Fossils from ancient sea creatures became embedded in the limestone as the mountain began to form, creating a fun surprise for the scientists who discovered them!

Humans found the deepest spot on Earth—and went there.

The Ring of Fire is also home to the deepest point on the planet: the Challenger Deep. It's located within the Mariana Trench, a banana-shaped valley deep under the Pacific Ocean. At its lowest point, the Challenger Deep is almost 7 miles beneath the surface. Obviously, when humans located it, we had to find out what was there!

The first successful dive to the bottom of the Challenger Deep happened in 1960, when oceanographers Jacques Piccard and Don Walsh took the *Trieste* submarine to the ocean floor. Amazingly, no one would follow in their footsteps until movie director James Cameron took the *Deepsea Challenger* to the bottom in 2012. Since then, there have been many more successful missions to the Challenger Deep, and our understanding of the ocean floor has increased quite a bit.

Point Nemo is the most remote location on Earth.

There is a point in the middle of the Pacific Ocean that scientists call Point Nemo. When you're standing on Point Nemo, you're the furthest you'll ever be from land. Point Nemo is approximately 1,670 miles away from the closest islands, making it one of the hardest to reach places on the planet. In fact, it takes its name from Captain Nemo, the submarine captain in Jules Verne's book *Twenty Thousand Leagues Under the Sea*.

Because Point Nemo is so remote, there are no major airline routes or shipping lanes that pass nearby. As a result, the closest humans to Point Nemo are sometimes the astronauts in the International Space Station orbiting overhead!

The Great Lakes hold 21% of the world's fresh water.

Most of the water on Earth is salt water. In fact, just 3% of the water on the planet is fresh water—and most of that is stored in frozen glaciers. Less than 1% of all water on Earth is actually drinkable, and about 21% of it is in the Great Lakes!

Only Russia's Lake Baikal contains more fresh water than the Great Lakes. Together, Lake Baikal and the Great Lakes contain almost half of the fresh water on Earth's surface. That's pretty impressive!

There are enormous impact craters hidden across Earth.

Earth isn't covered in craters the way Mars or the moon appear to be. This is partly because Earth has a thick atmosphere that causes most small rocks to burn up before they hit the surface. But sometimes, a rock slips through, leaving behind a pretty big crater.

These craters aren't always easy to find. Most of them are millions of years old, and they've been worn down by wind, rain, erosion, and other natural forces. But scientists can still detect the remains of these craters—and you might be surprised where they are!

The largest crater on Earth is the Vredefort impact structure, located in South Africa. Scientists estimate it was caused by a meteor impact that occurred roughly 2 billion (yes, *billion*!) years ago. The second largest is the Chicxulub crater, located under the Yucatán Peninsula in Mexico. This crater was caused 66 million years ago by the meteor scientists believe killed the dinosaurs.

Earth is 4.54 billion years old.

Earth is old—like, *really* old. But when exactly was the Earth "born"? It can be hard to put a date on it since the planet took a long time to fully form. In the early solar system, Earth started to form out of a rotating cloud of gas and dust. Around 4.5 billion years ago, that cloud came together to form the basic shape of Earth, but it wouldn't have been a very nice place to live. Early on, Earth was a ball of melted rock with no atmosphere (and definitely no water). Over time, Earth started to cool down, and about 3.7 billion years ago the first life forms began to arrive.

Pangaea isn't Earth's only supercontinent.

Roughly 300 million years ago, plate tectonics brought Earth's continents together to form the supercontinent of Pangaea. It may sound unusual, but the name *Pangaea* comes from the Greek word *pan* (meaning "all") and *gaia* (meaning "land"). The huge supercontinent stretched almost all the way from the North Pole to the South Pole and was surrounded by a superocean scientists call *Panthalassa*. Pangaea began to break up about 200 million years ago when the continents started drifting into the positions we know today.

You might be interested to know that Pangaea is not the Earth's only supercontinent. Millions of years before Pangaea came, *Pannotia*, a "short-lived" supercontinent that lasted less than 100 million years. Before that came *Rodinia*, a supercontinent formed around what is now North America.

The most powerful earthquake ever recorded caused tsunamis on the other side of the world.

In 1960, Chile suffered a magnitude 9.5 earthquake, the most powerful earthquake ever recorded. The quake was extremely destructive and released so much energy that it caused tsunamis as far away as Hawaii, the Philippines, and even Japan. That means those waves travelled more than 10,000 miles before finally striking land, which is pretty scary to think about. Today, we have warning systems in place to keep people safe after an earthquake. Hopefully, a tsunami won't take anyone by surprise in the future.

There are 10 million viruses in a single drop of seawater.

Don't worry, you won't wind up infected with a million mystery diseases if you swim in the ocean. While there are as many as 10 million viruses in every drop of sea-water, almost all of those viruses only affect bacteria and other microscopic life forms. Some of these viruses are pretty important, since they help make sure certain bacteria don't multiply too much and grow out of control. It's good to remember that microscopic life makes up a huge part of all life on Earth—there's a lot we can't see with the naked eye!

Earth may once have been completely frozen.

The Snowball Earth theory says that during one (or more) of Earth's ice ages, the planet may have gotten so cold that there was no liquid water left on the surface. That means every ocean, lake, and stream was frozen completely solid!

Not all scientists are convinced, though. A completely frozen Earth would probably kill all animal and plant life on the planet, which obviously didn't happen since we're still here! However, some scientists say basic forms of life could still exist under the ice, so the theory could still be true.

Myth Busters!

Mount Everest is the tallest mountain in the world.

Mount Everest is definitely the *highest* mountain in the world, but that doesn't necessarily mean it's the *tallest*. Hawaii's Mauna Kea is actually taller than Mount Everest.

Mount Everest is 29,032 feet tall *and* high. Mauna Kea is a whopping 33,481 feet tall. But, about 20,000 feet are underwater, and Mauna Kea only reaches about 13,000 feet above sea level. Maybe there are even taller mountains hiding under the sea!

Earth spins slowly. That's why we can't really feel it moving.

Actually, Earth spins incredibly fast. At the equator, it spins a whopping 1,000 mph! Of course, on the surface it doesn't feel like we're moving at all. There are a few reasons for this. The first is gravity, which holds us to Earth's surface. The second is a thing called relative motion. Since we're standing on the surface of Earth, we're moving at the same speed as Earth. Think of it like riding in a car: When you are in a car going 50 mph, it doesn't feel like you're moving that fast. That's because you and the car have the same relative motion. You only feel a change when you speed up or slow down, and the same is true on Earth. If Earth suddenly started spinning faster or slower, you would definitely notice!

Err, Bobby, I think we can just stand up

Quicksand isn't real.

Quicksand pops up all the time in movies and TV shows—especially cartoons. The idea of dangerous sand that can suck you underground is pretty scary. That leaves many wondering, *Is quicksand even real?* The answer is a surprising *yes!* But . . . quicksand isn't very dangerous. In fact, quicksand is denser than the human body, which means instead of being sucked under, you can float on top of it! Also, quicksand is usually just a few feet deep, so even if you fell into a pool of quick-sand, you could probably stand right up.

Fact or Fiction?

Gold comes from space.

Gold does not form naturally on Earth—which means all of the gold on the planet came from outer space. Scientists think a meteor shower roughly 3.8 billion years ago is what first brought gold to Earth, scattering it across the planet while it was still forming. Today, gold is usually found in areas with lots of volcanoes or earthquakes, because these allow the gold to rise back to the surface!

Fact!

Gold isn't the only element that comes from space. In fact, most elements that are heavier than iron are formed when a star goes supernova. These massive explosions are what send heavier elements into the universe, where they can make their way to planets, moons, asteroids, and even other stars. In fact, many of the elements that make up the human body are formed by supernova explosions. As astronomer Carl Sagan once said, "We are made of star-stuff!"

Rivers used to be so polluted that they could catch fire.

Pollution is dangerous for many reasons. When rivers, lakes, and other water sources get filled with toxic chemicals, they become less safe to drink. Sometimes, rivers can become so polluted that they can't be used for drinking water at all until they're cleaned up.

During the Industrial Revolution in the United States, a lot of pollution was dumped into rivers and streams. It got so bad that the Cuyahoga River, which runs through Cleveland, Ohio, actually caught fire more than 10 times! A river catching on fire is never a good sign, and these disasters helped the government realize they needed to take action to stop businesses from dumping chemicals in the water supply. Today, America's waterways are much cleaner, but we have to work to keep them that way.

The Appalachian Mountains and the Scottish Highlands were part of the same mountain range.

During the days of Pangaea supercontinent, there was a massive mountain range called the Central Pangaean Mountains. When Pangaea broke apart and the continents we know today began to form, that mountain range split up. The Appalachian Mountains in the eastern United States are one remnant of the Central Pangaean Mountains—and so are the Scottish Highlands in the United Kingdom, the Caledonian Mountains in Scandinavia, and the Anti-Atlas mountain range in Africa!

The Appalachian Mountains aren't very tall— at least not compared to a mountain range like the Rocky Mountains. That's because the Appalachians are extremely old and have been worn down by erosion over millions of years.

Snowflakes are their own parachutes.

Raindrops don't fall very fast, but snowflakes fall even slower. In fact, it takes the average snowflake about an hour to reach the ground after falling from the clouds. This is partly because unlike raindrops, snowflakes are wide and flat, which creates air resistance as they fall. That means snowflakes basically act like their own miniature parachutes! Snowflakes also have less mass than raindrops, and that mass is spread out over more space. That means they can be blown around by the wind much more easily, so their path to the ground isn't straight.

So, the next time you throw a snowball, just think about how long it took each of those flakes to wind up in your hand!

Earth is only 29% land.

If you've ever looked at a globe, you probably know that Earth is mostly covered by water. But you might be surprised to learn just how much water. In fact, 71% of the Earth's surface is covered by oceans and seas, which means just 29% is land!

Even though water is everywhere, most of it isn't drinkable. Scientists estimate that 97% of the water on Earth is salt water, leaving just 3% for humans, plants, and animals to drink. Fortunately, the water cycle helps replenish that fresh water. Today, people are also experimenting with ways to desalinate water (aka take the salt out) to make it drinkable. Hopefully our awesome technological advances will help us out!

PHYSICS & CHEMISTRY

Scientists worldwide have made fascinating discoveries that have changed the way we understand math, physics, and chemistry, and we've used those discoveries in incredible ways. We have completely eliminated some diseases, discovered penicillin, and determined exactly how many times a piece of paper can be folded. (Take a guess!)

Do you know who coined the term "radioactive"? Or that water can freeze *and* boil at the same time? Or that most of the universe is filled with only two gases: hydrogen and helium? Get out your lab coat and microscope and take a closer look at how strong gravity really is, the actual size of an atom, and whether or not there's gold in your TV.

Are you ready to find out once and for all what a proton tastes like?

Let's go make some chemistry!

Fact or Fiction?

The lead in your pencil is the same material as a diamond.

First of all, pencil "lead" isn't actually lead—it's graphite. But it's true that graphite and diamond are both made entirely from carbon atoms.

Fact!

Carbon is a fascinating element because its atoms can be arranged in many different ways. Temperature, pressure, and other things can affect the way carbon atoms are structured. Some of those structures, like graphite, are very soft. Others, like diamond, are very hard. This is because graphite is structured in "sheets" that come apart pretty easily, while diamonds have a rigid structure that makes them incredibly strong.

Sadly, the structure makes all the difference in this case—so don't bother trying to sell your pencil lead for a profit!

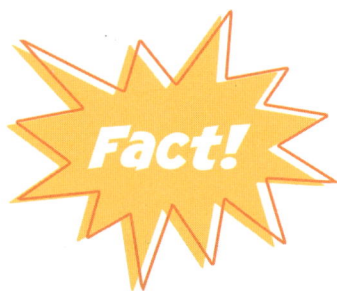

Metals are all silver-colored . . . except copper and gold.

Strange as it sounds, almost every metallic element on the periodic table has a silvery color. The only exceptions are copper, which is reddish-brown, and gold, which is, well, gold. Think about other metals like aluminum, platinum, titanium, lead—they're all silver. Why? Because of the atomic structure of these elements. Metals tend to absorb all colors of light equally. As a result, the light that bounces back to our eyes is a neutral, white-ish color that appears silvery to us. Gold and copper, on the other hand, absorb light differently. They reflect more colorful light back to our eyes.

This is part of the reason gold is so valuable: Even though gold is a soft, easily damaged metal, its color is unique. Copper is also valuable. It has natural properties that kill bacteria, viruses, and yeasts, which is why many houses have copper pipes!

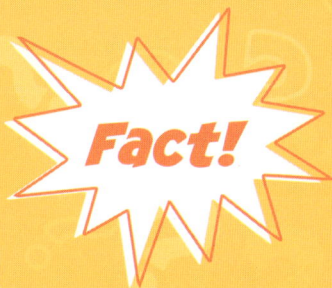

Fact!

Try It!

Want to taste a proton? Go for it.

Protons are the positively charged subatomic particles found in the center of an atom. But did you know you can detect protons all by yourself? It's true! Hydrogen ions (which are just single, freely-floating protons) are released from things that are acidic—and they make your food taste sour. The more protons in a food, the more sour that food will taste. Weird, right? Try it yourself at home: Bite into a lemon and let your "proton detector" (aka your tongue) do the rest!

If you add salt to water, the water level will go down. Seriously!

It sounds crazy, but if you pour a handful of salt into a glass of water, the water level will go down, not up. Why? It's complicated, but you can think of it like this: Salt molecules fit neatly into the gaps between water molecules, so when salt dissolves into water, it allows the water molecules to arrange themselves in a neater and more orderly way. As a result, the amount of water in the glass will appear to go down, even though the same number of water molecules are present. Try it and see for yourself!

Atoms are really, really small.

How many atoms thick do you think a sheet of paper is? 10? 100? 1,000? Well, the answer is somewhere between 500,000 and 1,000,000. It's true! A million atoms stacked on top of each other equals the thickness of one piece of paper!

Not all protons are the same shape.

Protons (along with neutrons and electrons) are sub-atomic particles that come together to form atoms. When you look at a diagram of an atom, protons are usually little spheres. But that's not always what they look like! In fact, there are four types of protons. Some look like spheres, but others look like peanuts. Some are oblong (like a football), and others look like little bagels! Protons are formed from quarks, and certain types of quarks give protons their different shapes. Pretty cool, right?

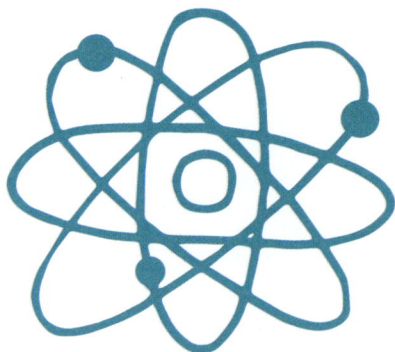

Heat causes the Eiffel Tower to get taller during the summer.

The Eiffel Tower is one of the most famous buildings in the world, and it's made almost entirely of iron. Like most metals, iron expands when it gets hot. This is thanks to an effect called thermal expansion, which causes matter to change its size at different temperatures. In fact, matter expands enough that engineers need to plan for it. They design metal bridges and other structures with thermal expansion in mind. How? They install special joints that account for a change in size.

Usually, the Eiffel Tower doesn't expand enough to be noticeable, but it's more than 1,000 feet tall. That's a lot of iron to expand. During the summer months, when the hot sun is beating down all day, the Eiffel Tower becomes about 6 inches taller!

Sound generates heat.

Sound is created when sound waves vibrate the particles in the air. When that happens, a little bit of energy is transferred, creating a small amount of heat.

Of course, we probably won't be cooking our food with sound waves any time soon. The amount of heat created by even the loudest sounds is very, very small. Still, it's kind of neat to think that if you yell at a plate of food, you're making it just a tiny bit warmer.

When matter and antimatter collide, they destroy each other.

Antimatter is basically the opposite of matter. Instead of positively charged protons, it has negatively charged antiprotons. Instead of negatively charged electrons, it has positively charged positrons. If matter and antimatter come into contact with one another, the result is an explosion that destroys them both completely! Theoretically, there should be equal amounts of both matter and antimatter, but the universe as we know it is almost entirely made of regular matter. Scientists aren't really sure why there isn't more antimatter out there—it's a mystery!

Fact or Fiction?

Cold water freezes faster than hot water.

In fact, hot water sometimes freezes faster than cold water. Weird, right? The first person to notice this was a Tanzanian high-school student named Erasto Mpemba, and scientists now refer to it as the Mpemba Effect.

Fiction!

It's important to note that the Mpemba Effect doesn't always happen—it only happens under certain conditions, which makes it hard to prove. Scientists also aren't sure exactly what causes the Mpemba Effect to happen, but they do have a few theories. Some say when hot water starts to evaporate, there's less water left to freeze, which speeds up the process. Others think when frost begins to form on top of cold water, it acts like a shield for the rest of the water and slows down the freezing process. There are other theories, too—but they can get pretty complicated!

Water can freeze and boil at the same time.

Usually, water freezes at 32°F and boils at 212°F. But that's not always the case: The freezing point and boiling point of water can change depending on how much pressure the water is under. In very, very low pressure (about 1/160th of Earth's normal atmosphere), the freezing point and boiling point become equal: At 32.016°F, water exists in all three states of matter (solid, liquid, and gas) at the same time. Scientists call this the triple point. Can you imagine seeing water boiling, freezing, and melting, all at the same time? Crazy, right?!

Fact!

Most materials have a triple point. Usually, triple point occurs at very low pressure, but there are some substances (like carbon and carbon dioxide) that require very high pressure to reach their triple point. There isn't any practical use for the triple point—it's just pretty cool to see something boil and freeze at the same time!

HOW IT WORKS

Sounds Change as You Move Toward or Away From Them

Have you ever noticed the sound of a siren (like an ambulance siren) changes as the siren goes by? This is because of something called the Doppler Effect, and it has to do with the way sound waves travel through the air.

When an object making a noise is moving toward you, the sound waves in front of that object "bunch up," which makes the sound seem higher pitched. When an object is moving away from you, the sound waves have the chance to spread out more, so the sound seems lower pitched. This is why an ambulance, or a train whistle, or even a revving engine will sound different as it passes by.

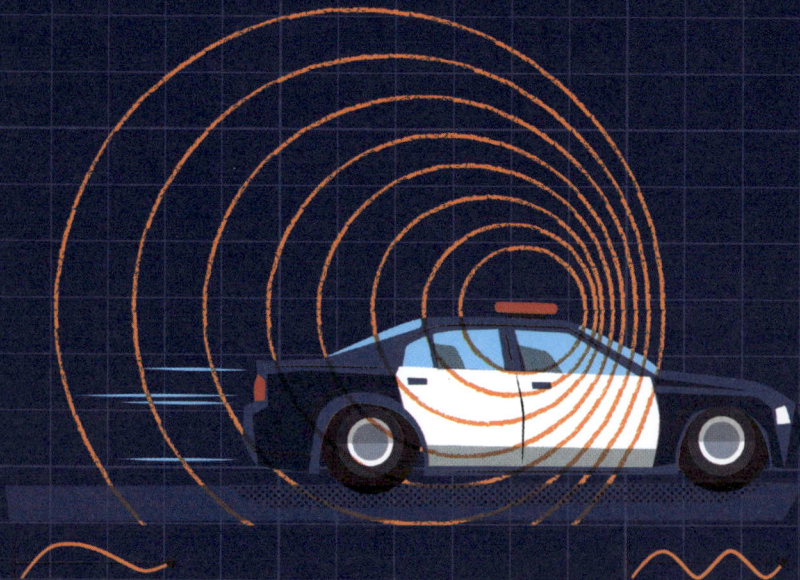

Light travels much, much faster than sound.

Nothing in the universe travels faster than light, which moves at a whopping 671 million miles per hour (mph). Sound, on the other hand is much slower. Want to guess how fast sound travels? Go ahead and think of your answer.

Okay, ready?

The speed of sound is . . . 767 mph. That means light is almost 900,000 times faster than sound!

That probably shouldn't come as a surprise: We can break the sound barrier (that's what causes a sonic boom), but nothing can travel faster than light. No matter what science fiction movies say, that's a barrier that can't be broken.

This is why thunder comes after lightning. The light from a lightning strike reaches your eyes almost instantly, but the sound of the thunder might take a few seconds to hit your ears.

Penicillin was discovered by accident.

Penicillin is one of the best antibiotics we have—and it was discovered completely by accident. In 1928, Scottish biologist Alexander Fleming came back from vacation to find that one of his petri dishes was growing mold, and that mold seemed to be stopping the nearby bacteria from growing. With a little extra effort, Fleming managed to turn that mold into a chemical that could kill bacteria (on purpose, this time). And thus, penicillin was born!

That's the amazing thing about chemistry. Sometimes, the most amazing discoveries happen completely by accident.

Fact or Fiction?

Humans have completely eliminated multiple diseases.

This might be one of our most impressive accomplishments. For hundreds of years, smallpox was one of the most dangerous diseases on Earth—but today, it has been completely destroyed. The last smallpox victim passed away in 1978, which means the disease has not killed a single person in almost 50 years!

Fact!

Smallpox is the only human disease that has been successfully destroyed, but we also eliminated a disease called rinderpest that infected cows, deer, buffalo, and other animals. This was a major problem for farmers, and the United States and other countries worked together to put a stop to the disease. In 2011, scientists announced that rinderpest was completely gone. As our understanding of medicine and chemistry improves, so does our ability to prevent diseases.

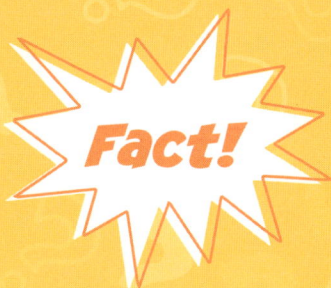

Reality Check!

Technically, everything you see is in the past.

Your eyes work by absorbing the light that reflects off everything around you. But light doesn't travel instantly: The speed of light is 186,000 miles per second. That means there is a slight delay between when the light bounces off an object and when it hits your eye—so what you're seeing is technically the past!

On Earth, the delay is too small to notice. But things are a little different in space. The stars in the sky can be hundreds of light-years away—and that means what we're seeing is the light those stars emitted hundreds (or thousands) of years ago.

Gravity isn't actually very strong.

The are four fundamental forces in the universe: strong and weak nuclear forces, electromagnetic force, and gravitational force. Of the four, gravity is by far the weakest. It actually makes sense when you think about it. Yes, gravity keeps us from flying off into space, but you can also defeat gravity by jumping in the air!

Even though gravity is weak, it has a much longer range than the other fundamental forces, which makes it seem stronger than it is. That's why the gravity of stars, planets, and other huge objects in the universe can affect each other even when they are light-years apart.

Color doesn't really exist.

An object isn't really "blue" or "red" or any other color. Color is just the way our brain makes sense of different wavelengths of light. So, the color we see depends on which wavelengths of light are absorbed by the object and which are reflected back at us. So, an apple isn't really red—that's just the color that bounces off it and into our eyes!

You can only fold a piece of paper seven times.

Paper is thin, right? So you might think it's easy to fold it in half a whole bunch of times. That's not true, though. Even something as thin as paper gets pretty thick once you start folding it! In fact, a standard piece of paper can only be folded in half seven times before it becomes thicker than it is wide—and then there's nothing left to fold. Scientists call this the Seven Fold Limit.

Of course, if you had a really big piece of really thin paper, you might be able to fold it a few extra times. In 2002, a California high-schooler named Britney Gallivan folded a piece of tissue paper in half 12 times, but the piece she started with was almost a mile wide!

Fact or Fiction?

There are more shuffle variations in a deck of cards than there are atoms in the Earth.

There are more ways to shuffle a deck of cards than you might think—about 8 followed by 67 zeros! That number is so big, it's hard to imagine. If you tried to count each possible shuffle— one per second—it would take you *trillions upon trillions of years*, far longer than the universe has existed. The universe is only about 14 billion years old. So if you shuffle a deck, chances are it's in an order that has never existed before in the history of the universe!

Fact!

That means that a deck of cards will be completely different every single time it's shuffled. In fact, you could spend billions of years just shuffling cards, and the odds are good that you'd never shuffle them the same way twice! Math can be pretty amazing, huh?

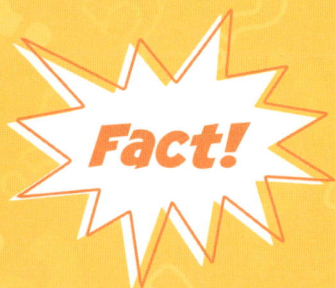

Marie Curie Was the First Woman to Win the Nobel Prize

Marie Curie was one of the most accomplished scientists to ever live. Not only was she the first woman to win a Nobel Prize, but she was also the first person to win a Nobel Prize twice—and she's still the only person to win Nobel Prizes in two different scientific fields! In 1903, she shared the Nobel Prize in Physics with her husband, Pierre Curie, and another physicist named Henri Becquerel for their work on radioactivity. (In fact, it was Marie Curie who invented the term "radioactive" in the first place!) Then, in 1911, she won the Nobel Prize in Chemistry after she discovered polonium and radium, two new radioactive elements.

Curie's work helped set the stage for advances in both engineering and medicine. Her study of radioactive elements led to breakthroughs in X-ray technology and cancer treatments, helping doctors do their jobs better. Her accomplishments also helped inspire millions of women to enter scientific fields, making her a role model for countless future chemists and physicists.

Radioactivity used to be measured in "sunshine" units.

When scientists were searching for a way to measure radioactivity in a person's body, the first thing they came up with was "sunshine" units. One sunshine unit is equal to the small amount of radiation we get from the sun, so a human who registers 10 sunshine units is 10 times more radioactive than normal. But since radioactivity can be scary and dangerous, some people thought the term sunshine units was inappropriate. Today, we measure radioactivity with strontium units, which measure the amount of radioactive strontium found in a subject's body.

Only two elements are liquid at room temperature.

Most elements exist as either a solid or a gas under normal conditions—only bromine and mercury are liquid at room temperature. You've probably seen mercury: It's a shiny, silvery liquid that looks kind of like a blob. Bromine, on the other hand, is a brownish liquid that just looks kind of disgusting. Both can be dangerous to touch with your skin, so even though mercury looks cool, you probably shouldn't handle it without gloves.

Fact or Fiction?

A "jiffy" is an actual unit of time.

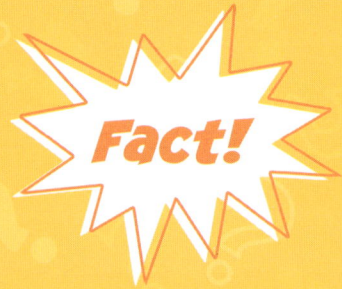

Fact!

If you've ever heard someone say "I'll be there in a jiffy," you probably thought it was a just a weird, made-up word. But a "jiffy" is a real scientific term! In fact, "jiffy" originally meant the amount of time it takes light to travel one centimeter (which, if you're curious, is about one trillionth of a second). This meaning has changed over time. Some scientists use "jiffy" to indicate the amount of time it takes light to travel one foot, and others use it for the amount of time it takes light to travel across the center of one atom.

Computer scientists also use "jiffy" to measure time, and some of them even invented a new term: the "mircojiffy", which is 1/65,536th of a regular jiffy. Now it's just getting silly!

Of course, most people don't use "jiffy" to mean any of those things. Most of us just know it means *fast!*

Nitroglycerin is used as a heart medication.

If you've heard of nitroglycerin (or "nitro"), it was probably in the form of TNT. Nitro is one of the primary ingredients in dynamite, which has been used in everything from coal mining to *Looney Tunes* cartoons for more than 100 years. But nitro isn't just good for opening mine shafts or catching the Road Runner: It's also a pretty good medicine!

When nitroglycerin is diluted (which basically means watered down), it can help treat heart disease, high blood pressure, and other medical issues. It's pretty cool that something originally used for destruction can serve such a positive purpose.

Fact or Fiction?

Not everyone on Earth experiences gravity in the same way.

There are places (usually very high points or very low points) where gravity becomes stronger or weaker. The further one is from Earth's core, the weaker gravity will be. Since Earth bulges slightly in the middle, a person standing on top of a mountain near the equator will weigh slightly less than a person on the ground. On the other hand, a person standing near the North or South Pole will weigh slightly more, thanks to the increased gravitational pull.

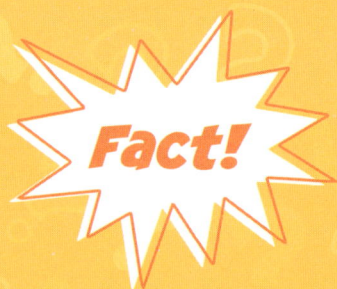

Fact!

It's not a huge effect, but it's there. Scientists say that if you suddenly teleported to the North Pole from the top of a mountain at the equator, you would lose about 1% of your body weight. That's not a ton, but you'd probably notice the difference!

The coldest place in the universe is on Earth.

The universe is cold, but it's not as cold as you might think. The cosmic background radiation of the universe means there is always a little bit of energy buzzing around. But on Earth, some crazy scientists have taken it upon themselves to see just how close to absolute zero they can get. (*Absolute zero is the coldest possible temperature—about -459.67°F or 0 Kelvin—where particles have minimal quantum motion.*) The answer? Pretty close! In 2017, researchers managed to cool a few atoms to just a few trillionths of a degree above absolute zero. It only lasted for 2 seconds, but for those 2 seconds that lab was the coldest spot in the entire universe.

Water is denser than ice.

The solid form of something is almost always denser than its liquid form. This makes sense, right? When a liquid becomes a solid, the molecules are packed more tightly together. But water is unique. In fact, it is the only common liquid that is denser than its solid form. This is why ice cubes expand when they freeze—and it's also why ice floats to the top of a glass of water!

Why does this happen? It's complicated. Ice has a crystal structure, which actually creates more space between molecules instead of less. There are other things with that sort of structure, but they are much less common than water—so you'll probably never run into them in your day-to-day life. Water really is special!

If something happened to the sun, we wouldn't know about it for 8 minutes.

It takes the light from the sun 8 minutes to reach Earth, which means if something happened to the sun, it would take 8 minutes for us to find out. Don't worry—nothing is going to happen to the sun (at least not for a few billion years). But just think: When we see a solar flare or a sunspot, we're actually seeing something that happened 8 minutes in the past.

Here's another cool fact: Gravity works at the speed of light. That means if the sun disappeared right now, Earth would continue orbiting the empty space for 8 more minutes!

There is probably gold in your television.

Gold isn't just valuable because it can be used to make expensive jewelry. It's also used in a lot of today's electronics. Gold is a "soft" metal, which means it can be easily molded into different shapes without breaking. It also lasts for a very long time and conducts electricity well, which means it's perfect for making televisions, laptops, phones, and other electronic devices. That means there's a good chance that if you cracked open your mobile phone, you'd find a small amount of gold in there making it work!

Glass is not exactly a solid.

If you've ever looked at an old window pane, you may have noticed it seems thicker at the bottom than the top, almost like the glass has melted. This is because glass isn't a solid—at least, not the way we normally think of solids. But it also isn't a liquid. Glass is what's known as an amorphous solid, which means while it appears to be a solid, it actually "flows" very slowly, almost like a liquid. It might take decades (or even centuries) before that flow is noticeable, but it's there.

No one can agree on how exactly glass should be classified, but "amorphous solid" seems to be the most popular answer.

Sometimes, a solid can turn straight into a gas.

Most of the time, a solid needs to turn to liquid before it can turn to gas. Take water, for example. When ice gets hot, it melts into water. When that water gets hot, it evaporates into gas. But sometimes a process called sublimation causes a solid to turn straight into gas without becoming liquid in between!

One good example of this is solid carbon dioxide (which we call dry ice). When dry ice is left out at room temperature, the solid evaporates directly into a gas! Sublimation is rare, but it's also pretty cool to watch.

When salt water freezes, it becomes fresh water.

If you froze salt water, you'd probably expect to wind up with salty ice cubes, right? Wrong! When water freezes, the crystal structure of the ice doesn't leave room for salt. Instead, it pushes the salt out. If you took a chunk of frozen salt water from the sea, it would taste almost as fresh as an ice cube from your freezer.

But please don't eat ice directly from the sea. Even though that ice won't be salty, it can still contain other chemicals and microbes that wouldn't be very healthy for you to eat!

Rubber tires are one giant molecule.

Rubber is a polymer, which means it is made up of long chains of repeating molecules. When rubber is made into tires, it is vulcanized, which means those polymers are linked together to make the rubber stronger. That also means a finished tire is one long chain of repeating polymers, which basically makes it one giant molecule! Since molecules are usually tiny, it's a little weird that one can be the size of a tire, but science is cool like that!

There is one temperature where Fahrenheit and Celsius temperatures are the same: -40°.

The two most common ways to measure temperature are the Celsius scale and the Fahrenheit scale. In America, the Fahrenheit scale is most common, but around the world most countries use Celsius. There are a few differences between them. For example, on the Celsius scale, water freezes at 0°C and boils at 100°C. On the Fahrenheit scale, water freezes at 32°F and boils at 212°F.

But there is one spot where both scales overlap: -40°. If the temperature ever reaches -40° and someone asks how cold it is, it won't matter which thermometer you look at—the answer will be the same!

The rarest element in nature is astatine.

Some elements, like hydrogen, nitrogen, or oxygen, are very common. Others, like gold or platinum, are pretty rare. But the rarest of all naturally occurring elements is astatine. Some scientists think there are only about 28 grams of astatine present on Earth at any given time, while others say it might even be less than 1 gram!

Astatine is formed when heavier elements break down, but once astatine forms it decays very quickly. That means even when scientists find natural astatine, they don't have much time to study it before it's gone. Thankfully, scientists can make their own astatine, which allows them to experiment with it. That's good news because some researchers believe astatine could be useful for certain medical treatments.

There are four elements all named after the same mine.

Nine different elements were discovered for the first time in Ytterby Mine in Sweden, and four of them were named after the mine. Yttrium, terbium, erbium, and ytterbium were all named after the place they were discovered.

Scandium, holmium, thulium, gadolinium, and tantalum are the five other elements discovered in the mine. Today, Ytterby is considered a historical landmark within Sweden, and it has even received a Historical Landmarks Award from the European Chemical Society in recognition of its contributions to elemental science.

Antimatter is the most expensive substance on Earth.

Antimatter is really hard to make, and it's even harder to keep it stable. Since matter and antimatter destroy each other when they touch, antimatter needs to be handled very, very carefully. Because of that, antimatter is pretty rare. In fact, scientists have only ever made a few nanograms of antimatter. Since a nanogram is 1 billion times smaller than a gram, that's not very much!

Scientists say a single gram of antimatter would cost roughly $65 trillion dollars. That's almost the value of the entire world economy combined! But unless our methods of creating and storing antimatter get a lot better, we probably won't be making anything close to a gram of antimatter anytime soon.

A lot of math symbols aren't as old as you think.

People have been doing math for a long, long time. So, you'd think symbols like + and - have been around forever, right? Wrong! The plus and minus signs weren't invented until the 1300s. Other symbols were even later. The = sign was invented in the 1500s, and the x for multiplication only came around in 1631!

Before that, people had to write out math equations by hand. Instead of 6 x 3, they would have to write "6 multiplied by 3". What a pain!

If two pieces of the same metal touch in space, they permanently fuse together.

Usually, fusing two pieces of metal together requires a lot of heat (think of a welding torch). But in space, things are a little different. In the vacuum of space, when two pieces of the same metal touch, they become permanently bonded. This process is called *cold welding.*

The reason for this is simple. On Earth, metals always have a thin layer of oxidation, which is a chemical reaction that happens when metal comes into contact with air, water, or other things that contain oxygen. In space, there is no oxygen—so there is nothing separating the atoms from each piece of metal. When they touch, there is nothing stopping them from fusing together and becoming a single object. This can actually be a problem: Astronauts have to be careful not to let certain pieces of metal touch!

Hydrogen and helium make up 99% of the universe's matter.

Hydrogen makes up roughly 75% of all matter in the universe. Helium makes up 24%, and the other 1% is made up of every other element on the periodic table combined. In a way, it's funny: Despite being the most plentiful elements in the universe, hydrogen and helium are both rare on Earth. Together, they make up less than 1% of Earth's mass.

Hydrogen and helium are both pretty simple, so it makes sense they would be more plentiful than other, more complex elements. Still, it's crazy to think that two gases make up 99% of the universe!

Helium was discovered in space before it was discovered on Earth.

Helium is the second element on the periodic table, and today it has a lot of different uses in science, medicine, and technology. But helium wasn't originally discovered on Earth: It was first found by scientists taking measurements of the sun during a solar eclipse. That also explains how it got its name: *Helios* is the Greek word for "sun."

Unfortunately, helium is a non-renewable resource. Since helium is lighter than air, it can easily float up and escape Earth's atmosphere, disappearing into space. We'd better make the most of the helium we have!

SPACE

It's hard to imagine just how big outer space is. It goes on for billions of light-years—and that's just the part we can see! Space is filled with all kinds of incredible and unbelievable things. There are stars billions of times bigger than our sun, black holes that suck up all light, and solar systems with not one, not two, but seven stars!

Have you ever wondered what the sun sounds like? Or how long a day is on other planets? Or what space smells like? In this section, you'll discover whether or not our moon is shrinking, and when (not if!) the Milky Way and Andromeda will collide.

Are you ready to meet the scientist who discovered dark matter and find out how long it's been since another star passed through our solar system? (Take a guess!)

Suit up and strap in! 3 . . . 2 . . . 1 . . . blastoff!

The footprints astronauts left on the moon will be there forever.

Well, *forever* might be a bit strong, but it's basically true: Those footprints will be there for millions of years. On Earth, wind, rain, erosion, and other natural forces change the shape of the land. If you leave a foot-print in the mud today, there's a good chance it won't be there tomorrow.

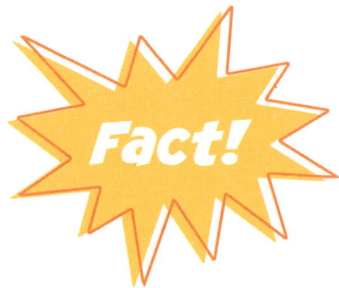

Fact!

But the moon is different. Since the moon has (basically) no atmosphere, there is no wind or rain to disturb the surface. That means the footprints astronauts have left there will probably be there forever—unless a meteor happens to strike that exact spot! That's just about the only way enough dust could be disturbed to fill in those footprints (well, unless another astronaut decided to scuff them out for some reason . . .).

Whatever happens on Earth, and whatever happens to humanity, there will still be evidence of what we accomplished millions of years from now.

The moon is shrinking.

But don't worry. Even though the moon is shrinking, it's happening very, very slowly. In fact, scientists estimate that the moon has shrunk about 150 feet over the last few hundred million years, so it won't be shrinking away to nothing anytime soon!

Fact!

What is making the moon shrink? The answer: The moon is still young, at least, compared to other planets and moons! The core of the moon is still cooling down from when it was first formed, and as it gets colder, it slowly shrinks. This causes the surface of the moon to shrink along with it, creating "moonquakes" and landslides that can last for a hours at a time. We can actually see "wrinkles" on the surface of the moon where the land is shrinking!

NASA scientists are worried that the moonquakes caused by the shrinking moon could make it dangerous for astronauts to land in certain places. Even though the moon is shrinking incredibly slowly, scientists still need to take this movement into account when planning future missions.

If we could see the whole Andromeda Galaxy, it would look six times bigger than the moon.

The Andromeda Galaxy is the closest major galaxy to the Milky Way. There are a few small, irregular galaxies (the Large Magellanic Cloud and the Small Magellanic Cloud), but Andromeda is a large, spiral galaxy like the Milky Way. Andromeda is roughly 2.5 million light-years away from Earth, which means it would take 2.5 million years to get there—even at the speed of light!

Because Andromeda is so far away, it isn't very bright in the night sky. Even so, it's still really, really big. In fact, if you could see all of Andromeda with the naked eye, it would look six times bigger than the moon! That's pretty amazing for a galaxy millions of light-years away.

Someday, the Milky Way and Andromeda galaxies will collide.

The Milky Way is slowly getting closer to its nearest neighbor, the Andromeda Galaxy. But don't fret—they won't meet for about 4.5 billion years. Even when they do, there isn't much to worry about. Astronomers say it is incredibly unlikely that any stars or planets would actually hit one another.

When they meet, the two galaxies will combine into a single, larger galaxy, and the gravity involved could create some interesting results. For example, there is a roughly 12% chance that our solar system could be thrown out of this new, combined galaxy entirely and sent spinning off into space! That sounds scary to think about, but scientists say even if it happened, the solar system would carry on the same way it always has and nothing much would change.

The number of stars we can see is shrinking.

The universe is expanding, and most galaxies are moving away from us. Billions of years from now, most of those galaxies will have moved beyond the edge of our observable universe, and their light won't reach us anymore. That means that someday, the night sky will be mostly empty, except for the stars within our own galaxy (and a few nearby galaxies that are linked to us by gravity). But that's not going to happen for a long, long time. And who knows? Maybe our understanding of the universe will have changed by then.

SuperSTAR Facts!

Some star systems have as many as seven stars.

In our solar system, we have just one star: the sun. But systems with more than one star are actually pretty common. In fact, one of our closest starry neighbors, Alpha Centauri, is a system that contains not one, not two, but *three* stars orbiting each other. That's not even the largest system. Scientists have discovered star systems with as many as *seven* stars! They say it may be possible for as many as eight stars to exist in a single system, but we haven't found any examples yet.

The more stars in a system, the more complicated it becomes. Systems with multiple stars can have planets, but it would be hard for life to evolve on them. With so many stars orbiting in such a chaotic way, the climate of a planet could change wildly over time, creating a difficult environment for life.

The North Star changes over time.

Today, the "North Star" is Polaris. But because Earth's axis has a slight "wobble" to it, that can change. Today, Earth's axis points directly at Polaris, but 5,000 years ago it pointed to a star called Thuban, and 13,000 years from now, astronomers say Vega will be the closest star to true north. That could be a good thing: Vega is a very bright star, which makes it easier to find in the night sky than Polaris. Unfortunately, it won't be as perfectly "north" as Polaris—it will be ever so slightly off. Still, it's cool to think about the North Star changing over time!

There are rogue planets without a star.

Planets usually orbit a star—but not always! Astronomers have discovered rogue planets that float freely on their own, without a star to guide them. These rogue planets sometimes form within a solar system before escaping, but other times they form on their own.

Astronomers say the Milky Way might have billions (or even trillions) of these rogue planets, and we've even found a few of them! The first rogue planets were discovered in 2000 by scientists from the United Kingdom, and more are expected to be found by NASA's Roman Space Telescope when it launches in 2026.

One teaspoon of a neutron star has as much mass as every human combined.

Neutron stars are incredibly dense. That means they have a lot of matter crammed into not a lot of space. In fact, a single teaspoon taken from a neutron star has roughly the same mass as every human on the planet!

A black hole is the only object in the universe denser than a neutron star. And black holes are formed in basically the same way: A neutron star is created when a star goes supernova but isn't quite big enough to form a black hole. Both black holes and neutron stars have incredibly strong gravitational pull, which is why they can pack matter together so tightly.

The sun is bigger than you think.

You probably know that the sun is the largest object in our solar system. But you might not know just how big it is. In fact, the sun makes up 99.86% of the solar system's total mass—that leaves just 0.14% for the rest of us!

Jupiter and Saturn are the largest planets, but even *they* seem tiny next to the sun. Compared to the sun, Earth is practically a speck of dust. It really puts things in perspective, huh?

Fact or Fiction?

The fastest-spinning star spins roughly 70 times per second.

It's actually even cooler than that. A pulsar called PSR J1748–2446ad (a seriously weird name!) is the fastest-spinning object ever detected, spinning an incredible 716 times every second! That means the surface of the star is moving at about 24% of the speed of light as it spins, making it one of the fastest objects in the universe.

Fiction!

Even normal pulsars are pretty cool. They are neutron stars that emit "beams" of energy from their north and south poles. If the pulsar is pointing the right way, we can detect those beams when they're pointed toward the Earth—like the light at the top of a lighthouse! Astronomers say there are certain types of pulsars that "pulse" so regularly they can keep time better than atomic clocks—the most accurate clocks we can make here on Earth.

About 70,000 years ago, another star passed through our solar system.

Stars can pass pretty close to each other, and astronomers say that's exactly what happened to our solar system 70,000 years ago. A small, red dwarf star called Scholz's Star (and its brown dwarf companion star!) passed through the edge of our solar system around that time, disrupting some rocky meteors and sending them hurtling toward the sun.

Sadly, red dwarf stars are extremely dim, which means Scholz's Star probably wouldn't have been visible from Earth, even when it was at its closest point. That's too bad, because 70,000 years isn't that long ago. It's fun to think of early humans looking up and seeing a new, red star in the sky!

WISE 0855–0714

Some stars are *actually* cool.

Brown dwarf stars are sometimes considered "failed" stars because they are too small for the powerful nuclear reaction that powers larger stars. That means that some of them can be cool—or even downright cold. The coldest star astronomers have ever found is called WISE 0855–0714 (someone needs to help them think of better names!), and it has a temperature of just 53°F. That means that if the gravity didn't crush you first, you could actually touch it!

If we could hear it, the sun would sound like a jackhammer.

We should all be grateful that sound can't travel in space. If it could, the sun would sound like a loud jackhammer running at all times, even though it's 92 million miles away! Thankfully, sound waves work by causing molecules to vibrate, and there aren't enough molecules in the vacuum of space for sound to travel. It just goes to show you how large and powerful the sun really is.

Space Is Smelly

Comets have a smell . . . and it's *bad*.

Comets are too far away for us to smell, but scientists can make a pretty good guess about their scent. We know most comets are made from things like hydrogen sulfide, ammonia, sulfur dioxide, and hydrogen cyanide . . . most of which smell pretty gross. Scientists say if a comet made of those materials was brought to Earth, it would smell like a terrible combination of lit matches, urine, and rotten eggs! It's not all bad, though. Hydrogen cyanide actually smells like almonds . . . so at least there's that?

There's a gas cloud 400 light-years away from Earth that smells like raspberries.

Sagittarius B2 is a gas cloud in the Milky Way situated almost 400 light-years away from the center of the galaxy. And Sagittarius B2 emits a chemical called ethyl formate, which—you guessed it—smells like raspberries! This particular chemical also smells like something else: an alcoholic spirit named rum. While this scent may not be everyone's cup of tea, it beats rotten eggs any day!

Space smells like cooked meat.

When astronauts return from a spacewalk or trip to the moon, their spacesuits and other equipment often have a smell. Buzz Aldrin said his suit smelled like "burnt charcoal" after walking on the moon. Fellow astronaut, Harrison Schmitt, described the smell as "spent gunpowder." But the most common description used by astronauts is "seared steak." Weird, right?

There is a reason space smells the way it does. Even though space is a vacuum, there are still all sorts of molecules floating around. Those molecules can cling to astronauts' spacesuits and react with the environment when they come back inside. The result can be pretty smelly—and might even make you hungry!

Black holes can get "stupendously" big.

Regular black holes are just called "black holes." Big black holes are called "supermassive black holes." Really big black holes are called "ultramassive black holes." But what happens when they get even bigger than really big? Scientists believe that black holes can be bigger than we ever imagined—and they call these black holes "stupendously large black holes," or SLABs for short.

It can be hard to measure the size of a black hole (they're usually very far away and hard to see), so scientists have only found one black hole they think may fall into the SLAB category. So far, the black hole at the center of the Phoenix A Galaxy (more than 8 billion light-years from Earth!) is the only one that fits the bill. Stupendous!

Black holes aren't actually "holes."

A black hole is what happens when a giant star goes supernova, then collapses into a single point called a *singularity*. Black holes are so dense, and their gravity is so strong, not even light can escape them. Every black hole has a ring around it called the *event horizon*, and once something crosses the event horizon, it can never come back. So even though black holes may look like holes, they're actually just very, *very* dense points in space!

The Woman Who Discovered Dark Matter: Dr. Vera Rubin

You probably don't know Dr. Vera Rubin—but you should. She was the first astronomer to find evidence that dark matter exists. While studying spiral galaxies, she saw that the stars at the edge of the galaxy's "arms" were moving faster than science said they should. Since they seemed to be defying the laws of gravity, Dr. Rubin determined there must be a different, invisible force acting on them. Today, we call this invisible "stuff" dark matter.

Dr. Rubin performed her work in the 1950s, 60s, and 70s, which was a difficult time for many female scientists. Today, many people in the scientific community believe she should have won the Nobel Prize for her discovery of dark matter but was held back because she was a woman. Whatever the case may be, Dr. Rubin inspired an entire generation of female astronomers, and she deserves to be a household name.

Fact or Fiction?

On Venus, a day is longer than a year.

A "day" is the length of time it takes for a planet to spin in a complete orbit once. A "year" is the time it takes a planet to travel all the way around sun. It takes Venus 243 Earth days to complete a full rotation, but just 225 Earth days to travel around the sun. That means a day on Venus lasts longer than a year!

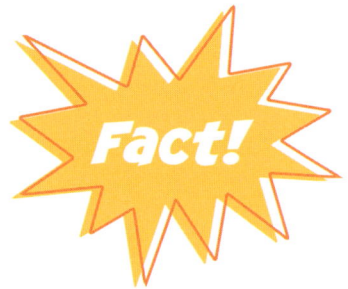

Fact!

Not only does Venus have the longest day/night cycle of any planet in the solar system, but it is also the only planet with a retrograde rotation. That means it rotates in the *opposite* direction from other planets. On Earth, the sun rises in the east and sets in the west. On Venus, it rises in the west and sets in the east. Scientists aren't sure what caused Venus to start rotating backwards. Some think it may have smashed into another planet while it was forming, and that changed its rotation. Others think the planet's thick atmosphere may have something to do with it. Whatever the case, it's exciting to have such an interesting planet right next door!

Jupiter's Great Red Spot has been around for thousands of years.

Nope. Not true. But it *has* been around for a long time. The Great Red Spot is an enormous storm in Jupiter's atmosphere that is roughly three times the size of the planet Earth. Even though a similar-looking storm was seen way back in 1665, astronomers now think that was a different storm, and the current Great Red Spot has only existed for about 190 years. It's hard to say for sure how long the storm will last. Some astronomers say it will probably last another 20 or 30 years; others say it could continue for hundreds of thousands of years.

Fiction!

No one knows for sure why the Great Red Spot is red, but it probably has to do with the chemicals in Jupiter's atmosphere. Despite its name, the Great Red Spot doesn't always stay the same color. Astronomers have watched it turn a pinkish color and even turn white occasionally.

HOW IT WORKS

Your Weight on Other Planets

Mass and weight are not the same. Mass refers to the amount of matter in an object, which does not change. Weight, on the other hand, measures the effect gravity has on an object—and that can change a lot. For example, an astronaut in zero gravity weighs nothing at all, even though their mass has not changed.

If you could stand on the surface of another planet, your weight would change quite a bit. For example, a person weighing 150 pounds on Earth would weigh just 30 pounds on the moon. This is because the moon is smaller and has less gravitational pull than Earth. On the other hand, a person weighing 150 pounds on Earth would way about 350 pounds on Jupiter. This is because Jupiter is much more massive than Earth, and the effect of gravity is greater. If that same 150-pound person could stand on the surface of the sun, they would weigh more than 4,000 pounds!

There might be a 9th planet in our solar system (no, not Pluto).

Astronomers believe there may be an undiscovered planet in our solar system, orbiting far beyond Neptune. They say this would help explain certain strange gravitational effects that they have observed on other objects in the solar system. However, the orbit of the proposed "Planet Nine" would be very, very far away from the sun, making it extremely difficult to locate. Until they can prove that it exists, Planet Nine will just be a theory.

Some astronomers have other theories. They say that instead of Planet Nine, there was once a fifth giant planet (like Jupiter, Saturn, Uranus, and Neptune) that was ejected from the solar system billions of years ago. Who knows where that planet might have ended up!

There might be as many as 2 trillion galaxies in the universe.

Astronomers say there are somewhere between 200 billion and 2 trillion galaxies in our observable universe—which means there might be even more we *can't* see! Since each galaxy has roughly 100 million stars, that means there are trillions upon trillions of stars out there. Even if just a small fraction of those stars has planets and a small fraction of those planets support life, that means there are probably other planets like Earth out there. Will we ever be able to contact those planets? Who knows, but it's fun to think about!

Marvellous Mars

Mars's moons are named "Fear" and "Dread."

Mars has two small moons, and scientists aren't sure how they formed. They're both pretty small and lumpy, unlike our nice, round moon. Since Mars is pretty close to the asteroid belt, some astronomers think it may have accidentally captured a pair of asteroids. Others think they might be left over from another planet colliding with Mars. Whatever the case may be, they're pretty unusual objects.

Astronomers named the moons *Phobos* and *Deimos*, which translate to "Fear" and "Dread." But have no fear—there's nothing evil about them. Phobos and Deimos were the sons of the Greek god Ares. Of course, you may know Ares better by his Roman name: Mars.

Mars is rusty.

Mars is known as "the Red Planet," but have you ever wondered how it got its famous color? It's actually because the surface of Mars is covered in a layer of iron oxide—which most people know as rust!

The Martian soil is rich in iron, and as iron is exposed to oxygen, it oxidizes, which causes the iron to rust. On the surface, the color isn't nearly as intense, but when dust storms kick all that iron oxide up into the atmosphere, the planet appears blood-red. No wonder it was named after the Roman god of war!

That's the third dust storm this week!

Mars has some extreme weather.

The atmosphere on Mars is about 100 times thinner than Earth's atmosphere, and about 95% of it is carbon dioxide, which humans can't breathe. But the fact that Mars has an atmosphere means it also has weather. In fact, Mars is famous for its high winds and dust storms, which can sometimes cover the entire planet for weeks or months at a time!

Like Earth, Mars has seasons, but they are more extreme than ours. Temperatures on Mars can be surprisingly warm (as high as 70°F), but also bone-chillingly cold (as low as -100°F). Since Mars is the most Earth-like planet in our solar system, scientists dream of someday changing the planet's climate to be more friendly to humans. But it's clear we have a long way to go!

Fact or Fiction?

The first human-made object in space was a manhole cover.

Fiction!

Believe it or not, a manhole cover may have been the *second* human-made object in space. The first thing humans managed to launch into space was a German test rocket during World War II. The *MW 18014* rocket reached a height of 109 miles in 1944, making it the first human-made object to cross over the line into what we consider "space."

But in 1957, a manhole cover took center stage. The United States was doing underground nuclear tests in the Nevada desert, and there was a small manhole cover over the area where one bomb was buried. When the bomb exploded, the cover was blasted straight up into the sky at roughly 125,000 miles per hour—making it the fastest human-made object ever recorded. The scientists never found the cover, and they say it was probably moving too fast to burn up in the atmosphere. That means somewhere out there in the solar system, a manhole cover is probably still blazing across the sky!

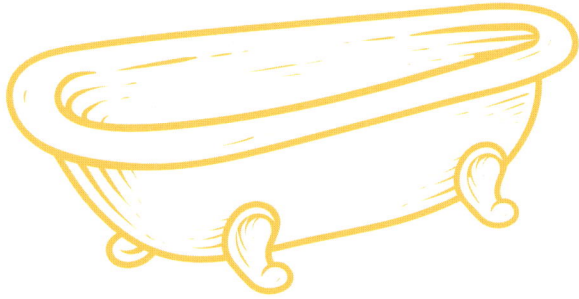

If you put Saturn in a bathtub, it would float.

Saturn and Jupiter are the two gas giants in our solar system (Uranus and Neptune are considered ice giants). They are made up mostly of hydrogen and helium gas, which means they are not very dense. In fact, Saturn is the only planet in the solar system less dense than water, which means if you could find a big enough bathtub, Saturn would float in it! Sadly, Jupiter is almost twice as dense as Saturn, so it would sink straight to the bottom.

Saturn's rings are not solid.

Even though they look solid from Earth, Saturn's rings (and the rings around Jupiter, Uranus, and Neptune, for that matter) are actually just billions of pieces of rock and ice orbiting the planet. Some of those particles are the size of a grain of sand, while others can be the size of boulders. Saturn even has a couple of moons that rotate *inside* its rings! Close up, the rings probably wouldn't look like much—but when you see them from a distance, they are stunning.

Mars will probably have rings someday.

Phobos, one of Mars's moons, is slowly but surely falling out of the sky. Scientists say that in about 50 million years, Phobos might crash into the surface of Mars . . . or will it? Some astronomers think that instead of crashing into the planet, Phobos will be torn apart by gravity and break into millions of tiny pieces. If that happens, those pieces will scatter into orbit and eventually form rings. It would be pretty cool to look up into the night sky and see rings around our closest neighbor.

Mars is a geological wonder.

Earth has some truly spectacular features, but these natural wonders can't even come close to the ones on our neighbor planet, Mars.

Mars is home to the tallest mountain in the solar system: Olympus Mons. This massive mountain stands roughly 72,000 feet tall—two-and-a-half times the height of Mount Everest! But that's not all. Mars is home to the largest canyon in the solar system, too. The Grand Canyon's 277 miles may seem like a lot, but the canyon Valles Marineris stretches almost 2,500 miles across the Martian landscape, becoming nearly 4 miles deep in some places. It's almost as wide as the entire United States.

With any luck, humans will someday walk the surface of Mars. Imagine being the first person to lay eyes on these incredible natural features!

Uranus rotates on its side.

Uranus has a pretty unusual feature: Unlike the other planets in the solar system, it rotates on its side. That means Uranus's north pole doesn't point up—it points toward the sun! While the other planets spin like a top, Uranus "rolls" on its side during its journey around the sun. The fact that Uranus has rings makes this look especially cool: Unlike Saturn's rings, which look like a belt around the planet's middle, Uranus's rings run straight up and down.

Astronomers think another planet (or another massive object) ran into Uranus sometime in the distant past, knocking it on its side and causing this strange rotation. We'll probably never know for sure what hit it, though—it was just too long ago.

A supernova can outshine an entire galaxy.

When a big star reaches the end of its life, it triggers a massive explosion called a *supernova*. These supernovas (or *supernovae*) release a lot of energy and can shine brighter in the sky than entire galaxies for a little while. Some can be even brighter than that. In 2016, astronomers spotted a supernova that was 20 times brighter than all the stars in the Milky Way combined. Wow!

Supernovas are bright, but they also don't last very long. The explosion itself takes just a few seconds, but the light from the supernova will remain bright for weeks or months. That might sound like a long time, but on a cosmic scale it's practically nothing.

Some moons have oceans.

There are a few moons in our solar system that scientists think could have liquid water. Astronomers say Jupiter's moon, Europa, may have an ocean under its surface that contains more water than all of Earth's oceans combined! Saturn's moon Enceladus also has an underground ocean, and astronomers have seen giant geysers of water shooting into space from the surface. These are just two of the many moons (and other objects) in the solar system that may contain water.

Water is one of the basic building blocks of life, which means these moons are among the most likely candidates for alien life. Don't worry, we're not going to find little green men on Europa—but we could find some new bacteria!

Saturn has 146 moons . . . and counting!

Mercury and Venus have no moons. Earth has one. Mars has two. The further out you go in our solar system, the more moons planets seem to have. For instance, Jupiter has 95 moons, and Saturn has a whopping 146 (so far!). Some of those moons, like Titan and Enceladus, are pretty big. But most are tiny and are probably just small asteroids that Saturn managed to capture within its orbit.

When it comes to Saturn, deciding what counts as a "moon" can be hard. Some of its 146 moons are so small, they aren't much different from the chunks or rock and ice that make up the planet's rings. That means new moons are constantly being discovered and reclassified. Who knows—by the time you read this book, maybe scientists will have found even more!

The moon is further away than you think.

When you look at pictures of the solar system, Earth and the moon always look very close together. But in reality, the moon is 238,900 miles away. That probably doesn't mean much to you, so think of it this way: If you lined up every planet in the solar system (even the big ones like Jupiter and Saturn), they would all fit in the space between Earth and the moon!

Asteroid fields aren't actually that dangerous.

If you've seen movies like *Star Wars* or shows like *Star Trek*, you've probably seen an asteroid field (or asteroid belt). They usually involve huge numbers of space rocks zooming around wildly, smashing into each other and causing chaos for the explorers just trying to make their way to safety. It's fun and exciting, but there's just one problem: That isn't *quite* how asteroid fields look.

In reality, the asteroids in the belt around the sun are usually hundreds of thousands of miles apart—which means they almost never run into each other. The total mass of the asteroid belt isn't very impressive. Even if you somehow mashed together every asteroid in the belt, they would only add up to about 3% of the mass of the moon. So, the next time you see a spaceship whizzing through asteroids in a movie, you'll know it's just for excitement.

Space junk is becoming a real problem.

Did you know that the space around Earth is littered with trash? Scientists say there are around 100 trillion pieces of space junk (mostly the remains of old satellites) trapped in low Earth orbit, with a total mass of almost 6,000 tons. This stuff is dangerous: Almost all of it is moving at 18,000 miles per hour, which is several times faster than a bullet. If it were to hit a satellite or a spaceship, it could be a major disaster.

Unfortunately, there are no international laws that say how space junk should be dealt with. Sometimes, pieces of debris will fall out of orbit and burn up in the atmosphere, but this doesn't happen often enough to be a real solution. The United States, China, and other countries have some ideas for solving the problem, but none of them have been put into action. For now, most countries are just focused on not making the problem worse.

Fact or Fiction?

Asteroids can have rings.

Everyone knows Saturn has rings, and most people know the other outer planets (Jupiter, Uranus, and Neptune) do, too. But planets aren't the only space objects that can have rings. Moons can have them, too. In fact, scientists think a few moons in our solar system might have faint ring systems. Weirdest of all, even rocks as small as asteroids can have rings!

Fact!

Astronomers have discovered a few ringed asteroids in our solar system. An object called 2060 Chiron is the smallest known object to have a ring system. It orbits the sun between Saturn and Uranus, and some scientists consider it a comet—making it the only known comet with rings. There are three other "minor" planets with rings: Quaoar, Chariklo, and Haumea.

Don't you wish Earth had rings, too? It doesn't seem fair that tiny asteroids get to enjoy beautiful rings, but we don't!

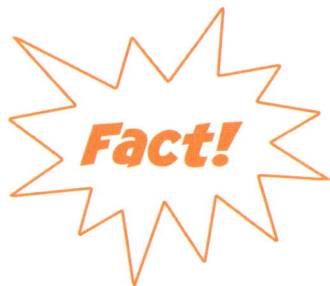

The first animal in space was a dog.

The first animal sent to space wasn't a human—it was a dog named Laika. In 1957, the Soviet Union sent Laika to space inside the Sputnik 2 satellite, and she became the first living creature to orbit the Earth. This was at the height of the space race between the United States and the Soviet Union, and the fact that the Soviets sent a living creature to space first really ruffled some feathers! It made the US work even harder on its own space program.

Fact!

In 1961, the US sent a chimpanzee named Ham to space. In 1963, France sent a cat named Félicette. And in 1968, the Soviets sent a pair of turtles all the way to the moon! Of course, the turtles didn't land on the moon—they just flew by and returned to Earth, where they landed a-okay in the Indian Ocean.

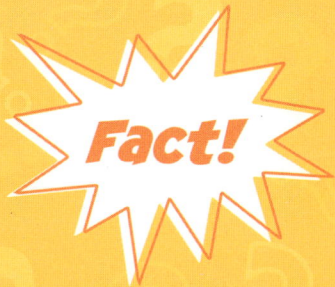

TECHNOLOGY & ENGINEERING

Get ready to discover some of the most impressive feats of science and engineering that humans have ever accomplished! Sometimes, science isn't just about discovery—it's about harnessing knowledge and creating something new. Humanity has produced remarkable inventors over the years, like the father of modern electricity, Nikola Tesla. We've built truly stunning creations, like the iPhone, which is more powerful than the Apollo spaceship's computer. From the Roman aqueducts to the first computer virus, humans have been inventing new things for thousands of years!

Have you ever wondered about the first video game ever invented? Do you know who computed all the math equations that enabled humans to land on the moon? What object is more common: a toilet or a mobile phone? From the earliest video calls to the invention of paper, this section is packed with cool facts about how we travel and communicate, and it even includes some predictions about the future of technology!

Are you ready to be impressed? Hang on to your helmets!

The QWERTY keyboard was designed to force people to type more slowly.

This is a popular rumor, but it isn't true. One of the biggest problems with early typewriters was that when two keys close together were typed in succession, the machine would sometimes jam. Since the QWERTY keyboard separates some of the most common letter combinations (like "th" or "he") by placing them further apart, most people believe this keyboard was designed to stop those jams from happening. In reality, there is no evidence that the QWERTY keyboard was ever supposed to slow typists down.

Fiction!

The QWERTY keyboard layout is still the standard layout for today's computers, but some people prefer other options. The Dvorak layout (named after inventor August Dvorak) supposedly requires less finger movement. The Colemak layout builds on the QWERTY layout but claims to be more efficient. The Workman layout tries to make each finger movement more comfortable. Ultimately, the QWERTY layout is popular for a reason, and it's probably here to stay.

The first computer was built almost 2,000 years ago.

This might be the most unbelievable fact in the entire book, but it's true. The Antikythera Mechanism was discovered in a shipwreck off the coast of Greece in 1901. The device itself contains a number of gears and markings that helped archaeologists figure out what it was originally used for—and that it was made almost 2,000 years ago! Thankfully, modern technology allowed archaeologists to use X-ray scans to peek inside the device without damaging it more. They found that it was a hand-powered model of the solar system that could predict things like eclipses and even the location of the planets! Scientists consider this to be the first example of an analog computer (not to be confused with today's *digital* computers).

The Greeks were known for their scientific advancements, but nobody knew they were capable of building something this complex!

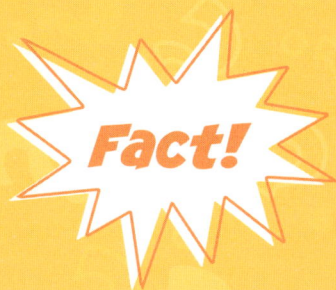

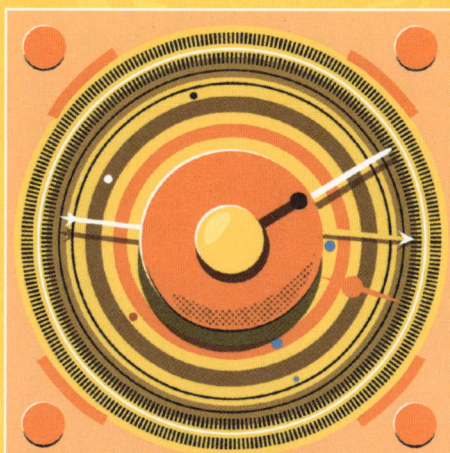

Watch Out!

The first computer virus was created in 1971.

In 1971, a programmer named Bob Thomas created "the Creeper," which most people agree was the world's first computer virus. He created the program as an experiment to see if a program could be taught to make copies of itself . . . and boy, did it succeed! Luckily, the Creeper virus didn't cause any damage, but when it infected a new system it would display the words, "I'M THE CREEPER. CATCH ME IF YOU CAN!" on the screen. Kind of funny, huh?

One of the earliest computer "bugs" was caused by an actual bug.

In 1947, two early computer programmers found an issue with one of their machines. When they looked inside it to find the cause, they found a live moth strapped in the machine! They pinned the moth into the log book with the note: "First actual case of bug being found."

Bugs get trapped in computers and other devices more than you might think. Computers are usually warm, which can make them seem like ideal shelter for a bug looking to get out of the cold. They don't usually cause any harm—it's just gross to think about!

To Google or Be Googled?

People use Google more than 8 billion times per day.

Google doesn't release official statistics, but researchers estimate that the search engine handles a little more than 8 billion searches per day. That's roughly 100,000 searches per second—and more than 2 trillion per year!

Want to hear something funny? One of the most common words people search for on Google is . . . *Google!* That's right. People type *Google* into Google to find . . . Google.

Google is named after a number called a googol, which is a 1 followed by 100 zeros.

Google is the most popular search engine in the world, and it helps people search billions of websites to find the information they need. Since Google searches through such a huge amount of information, the founders decided to name the company after the biggest number they could think of: the googol, which is a 1 followed by 100 zeros. Scientists think that's far more than the total number of atoms in the universe! But when one of the founders went to register the domain name, he accidentally spelled it "Google" instead of "Googol." It was a simple mistake—but it stuck. In the end, it probably worked out for the best. "Google" is easier to read and easier to say.

Nikola Tesla tried to build a "death ray."

Nikola Tesla is one of the most famous inventors of all time. For many years, he was Thomas Edison's greatest rival, but he never quite became as famous or successful as Edison. Still, he invented a lot of important technology that helped us improve things like radios, remote controls, neon lights, and certain electric systems. When he died, Tesla was working on his biggest invention yet: the "death ray."

Tesla claimed his death ray was an energy weapon that would be able to defeat entire armies and shoot planes out of the sky. When Tesla died, in the middle of World War II, everyone involved in the war scrambled to get their hands on his death ray plans! Needless to say, no death ray was ever built, which is probably for the best. Tesla wasn't the first inventor to think of a death ray, and he probably won't be the last.

You'll never believe when the sewing needle was invented.

You might not realize it, but one of the most important inventions in history was the sewing needle. Before the sewing needle, humans had no way to make clothes that actually fit properly—they could only drape themselves with animal furs large enough to cover them. That might sound cozy, but imagine trying to run after a buffalo with a heavy blanket draped over you!

If you had to guess when the sewing needle was invented, what would you say? A thousand years? Two thousand years? Well, the truth is even more incredible. Archaeologists say the oldest sewing needle ever discovered dates back roughly 61,000 years! It's amazing to think that humans have been making fitted clothes since before the dawn of civilization.

Driving in Circles: The One-Wheel Car.

Cars have four wheels. Bikes have two. But have you ever seen a vehicle with just one? In the 1930s, an inventor named John Archibald Purves built a one-wheeled car called the Dynasphere! It was basically a giant wheel with a driver's seat stuck right in the middle—so when the wheel rolled, the driver rolled too!

The Dynasphere looked futuristic, but it had some pretty big problems. The driver had to lean way out to one side just to see where they were going. The seat would sometimes spin around inside the wheel, making the driver feel like a hamster on a wheel! Inventors are always testing wild ideas—and the Dynasphere proves it, even if it didn't quite work out.

Fact or Fiction?

China invented paper hundreds of years before Europeans got around to it.

Actually, it would be fair to say Europeans never got around to it. Paper only made its way to Europe when Western armies, after fighting with Chinese troops, brought back knowledge of this incredible new material. While paper was invented in China around 105 AD, the first European paper mill didn't open until 1120 AD—more than 1,000 years later!

Fact!

Ancient China gave the world a lot of amazing inventions. In addition to paper, they invented the compass, gunpowder, and even early printing techniques!

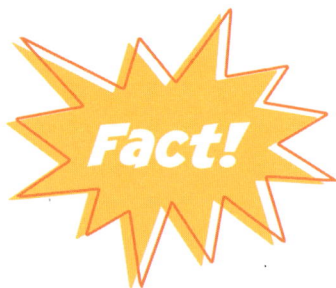

The steam engine was invented during the Middle Ages.

Fiction!

Actually, the first designs for the steam engine go back much, much further than that. Hero of Alexandria (yes, Hero was his name!) published designs for an early steam-powered engine called Hero's Engine sometime around 100 AD. That's almost 2,000 years ago!

A few prototypes based on Hero's Engine were built around that time, but they didn't really catch on. It wasn't until the 1500s, when the steam turbine was invented, that people began to see how useful steam power could be. In the late 1600s, the first steam-powered water pump was built, and then it was off to the races. Inventors soon got to work on the engines that would eventually power steam trains. These trains changed travel over land, making it much easier (and safer) to cross huge distances. Hero of Alexandria would be proud.

The Soviet Union invented a water computer.

In 1936, a Soviet scientist named Vladimir Sergeevich Lukyanov invented a computer that worked by carefully moving water through different pumps and chambers. The computer could measure how much water was in each container and how quickly the water was moving through the tubes. Then the computer used that information to perform complicated math. It might sound crazy, but it was actually pretty advanced! For a while, it was only the computer in the Soviet Union that could solve certain types of equations.

Unfortunately, a water-based computer isn't very efficient. Today's digital computers blow this computer out of the water (pun intended). It goes to show just how creative scientists can be when it comes to solving problems and inventing new technologies!

The first video game was created in 1952.

Created by computer scientist Alexander S. Douglas in 1952, *OXO* was the first video game. Different militaries around the world had computer programs that could simulate battle planning, but those weren't games— the public could play. *OXO* let players play tic-tac-toe against a computer, and it was the first game that included visuals for the players. Sadly, Douglas created the game as part of his college thesis, and it was thrown away afterward. It would be pretty cool to give it a try today!

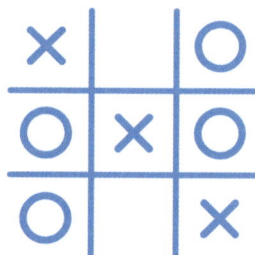

Glasses have been around for hundreds of years.

We take eyeglasses for granted, but they're actually pretty complicated. Think about it: a piece of glass made specifically for your eyeballs that lets you see better? When you really think about it, that's crazy! But what's even crazier is that people have been making glasses for hundreds of years. The earliest record of glasses dates back to the late 1200s in Italy, but glasses might go back even further than that. There is some evidence that monocles were being used in China as far back as 960 AD!

Even before glasses, people understood that glass could help people see. Around the year 1,000 AD, people began using "reading stones" to make text appear larger and easier to read on the page. Pretty cool, right?

Someday, we may be able to build a Dyson Sphere.

A Dyson Sphere is an idea for a megastructure that a scientist named Freeman Dyson had. Dyson wanted to think about how an extremely advanced civilization would get enough energy to power all of its technology. He thought if a species became advanced enough, they would build a giant, hollow ball around their sun so they could capture all of its energy. While the idea of a Dyson Sphere became popular in science fiction stories, actually building one would be pretty difficult. Builders would probably have to take apart entire planets to get enough material!

It's hard to say whether humans will ever be able to build a Dyson Sphere, but astronomers do keep an eye out for megastructures when they look for alien life.

Fact or Fiction?

The first alarm clock could only ring at 4 a.m.

Mechanical alarm clocks are older than you might think. The first one was invented way back in 1787, and it was made mostly of wood and brass. Inventor Levi Hutchins wanted a clock that could wake him for his morning prayers (or to go to work, depending on who you ask), so he created a clock designed to ring at 4 a.m. every day. Unfortunately, the alarm could never be adjusted—so 4 a.m. was the only time it could ever ring!

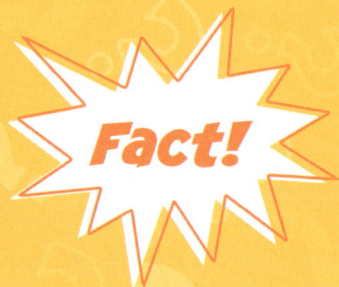

Fact!

Before mechanical alarm clocks, people managed to wake themselves up in other, more interesting ways. In Egypt and Greece, "water clocks" would slowly drip water into a container over time. When it reached a certain level, it could trigger a sound. In China, "candle clocks" would burn down until a pin was released from the melted wax. It would then drop onto a metal plate to create a loud ringing sound. Of course, these methods were not as exact as mechanical clocks. You'd have to know exactly how much water or wax to use if you wanted to wake up at a certain time!

The first webcam was invented to watch . . . a coffee pot?

It's true! In 1991, employees in the University of Cambridge computer lab were tired of heading to their break room only to find an empty pot of coffee. (That's just rude—when you finish a pot of coffee, the polite thing to do is to start brewing a new one!). In order to enforce that rule, the brilliant computer scientists in the lab rigged up a camera they pointed directly at the coffee pot. They made sure the video could be seen by everyone on the network, and *voilà*! No more coffee crimes.

HOW IT WORKS

Concrete is the Foundation of Modern Construction

You've probably never thought twice about concrete. It's all around us. It's used to make walls and floors. It's used to pave roads and parking lots. It's used to build bridges and dams.

Concrete is the most popular building material in the world, and one of the most useful. This is because concrete is incredibly strong, but it can also be molded into a lot of different shapes. It's also very stable and can support a ton of weight. Modern construction uses a combination of concrete and rebar (aka strong, metal rods) to make sure weight is spread out evenly across the columns of very tall buildings so that all the weight of the building doesn't crush the first floor. If you've ever wondered how skyscrapers can be so tall without collapsing, now you know.

Concrete has been around longer than you might think. Archaeologists have found evidence of early forms of concrete being used as far back as 6,500 BC, but the most well-known concrete users were the Romans. They began using a type of volcanic ash called *pozzolana* to make concrete around 300 BC, and they kept using it for hundreds of years. Many of those old Roman buildings are still standing today—which goes to show just how valuable concrete really is!

Siri's voice belongs to a real person.

Siri, Apple's famous digital assistant, originally had just once voice—and it belonged to Susan Bennett, a well-known voice actor. Bennett didn't actually know that she was the voice of Siri until friends and coworkers started asking her about it. The original recordings of her voice had been made years earlier as part of a totally different project. Apple later used those recordings, and Bennett was the voice of Siri until Apple updated the service in 2013.

Star Trek inspired the invention of the cell phone.

Martin Cooper usually gets credit for inventing the modern cellular phone—and he says *Star Trek* inspired him to do it. Cooper remembers watching Captain Kirk uses his communicator to call for help and wondering why we couldn't do the same. While the earliest cell phones were large, bulky, and ugly (Cooper called the first model the brick), they would get smaller and sleeker over the years. By the time cell phones became common, flip phones were the most popular model—which means they looked almost exactly like Captain Kirk's original communicator!

Internet Beginnings!

The first "spam email" was sent in 1978.

In 1978, a marketing manager named Gary Thuerk sent an email to about 400 people advertising a new computer. People were pretty annoyed, but apparently it worked, and Gary made a few extra sales. Unfortunately, it also made Gary the father of one of the most annoying parts of modern life: spam messages! Today, researchers estimate that almost 50% of all email is spam, with 160 billion spam messages sent every single day. Sorry, Gary—this probably isn't what you wanted to be remembered for!

You could make a video call in the 1930s.

Services like Zoom and FaceTime are common today, but you probably didn't know that video calling dates all the way back to the 1930s! A German inventor named Dr. Georg Schubert debuted a "visual telephone system" in 1936, and video call booths popped up in European cities over the next several years. Unfortunately, the start of World War II led to the technology being scrapped. The next attempt at two-way video calling didn't come until 1959, when Bell Telephone Laboratories began developing the Picturephone. Who knew video calls are almost as old as television?

The internet is older than you think.

The internet first started to look like the internet we know today in 1989, when the World Wide Web first went public. But most people agree the internet was "born" in 1983, when the ARPANET research project switched to a new standard that allowed it to connect to different networks.

ARPANET was basically the internet *before* the internet. As early as 1973, computer scientists were looking for ways to connect different devices. They wanted to make a "network of networks," which is a pretty good description of the internet today. You couldn't use ARPANET to check the latest sports scores or click through YouTube videos, but you could use it to talk to other computers—and that was pretty amazing at the time! Of course, once everyday people could access the internet, it really took off. Today, researchers estimate that there are a whopping 1.5 billion websites on the internet!

The first website launched in 1991.

Computer scientist Tim Berners-Lee launched the very first website on August 5, 1991. At that point, the internet had been around for a little while, but publicly accessible websites hadn't popped up yet. Tim's website was an educational one: It mostly just contained information on what he called the *World Wide Web Project*—which is basically what the internet would become! In fact, the "www" that starts most websites stands for World Wide Web.

The can opener was invented almost 50 years after the can.

Metal cans (originally made from iron and tin) were invented in 1810 to help store and preserve food more effectively. But the can opener wasn't invented until 1858, when inventor Ezra Warner patented the technology. What gives?

A can opener isn't the only way to open a can—it's just the most convenient. Before can openers were invented, people had to pop open their cans with a hammer and chisel, which was effective but not easy. Even worse, the hammer and chisel method isn't very precise, and could spill or contaminate the food inside the can. The can opener gave people a safe and easy method to cut through the top of a can without risking life and limb or upsetting the contents. Eventually, around 1920, the modern wheel-crank can opener design we know today became common. Not much has changed since!

The lighter was invented *before* the match.

It sounds crazy, right? But it's true—and the reasons make sense. Modern matches are actually pretty complicated. They're made using chemicals like red phosphorus and designed to light only under the right circumstances. On the other hand, lighters are relatively simple. All you really need is a flammable gas and something to create a spark.

German chemist Johann Wolfgang Döbereiner invented the first lighter in 1823, while the first friction match was invented by English chemist John Walker in 1826.

Voyager 1 is the furthest man-made object from Earth—and we can still talk to it.

Voyager 1 was launched in 1977, and its mission was to fly past Jupiter and Saturn to study the planets and their moons. Eventually, the probe left the inner solar system entirely.

But that's not the impressive part. The impressive part is that, almost 50 years later, Voyager 1 is still sending back data for scientists and astronomers to examine. Even though the probe's original mission was only supposed to last for 5 years, the probe was so well built that its electronic parts are still working decades later!

Katherine Johnson, Dorothy Vaughan, and Mary Jackson Helped America Win the Space Race

It took a lot of people working together to land a rocket on the moon, but not all of them got the credit they deserved. Katherine Johnson, Dorothy Vaughan, and Mary Jackson were NASA mathematicians during the 1960s, working as "human computers" to perform the complicated mathematical equations needed to plan a route to the moon. They were also African American women, which meant they faced a lot of discrimination during their careers. Thankfully, they didn't give up on their work. Instead, they were a really important part of the space race, helping the United States beat the Soviet Union to the moon.

All three women went on to have long and successful careers with NASA, earning the respect of their coworkers and eventually being promoted to supervisor positions. Eventually, the important role they played in the space program was recognized: In 2016, the book *Hidden Figures* told their stories. That same year, the book was adapted into a movie, also called *Hidden Figures*. Today, Katherine Johnson, Dorothy Vaughan, and Mary Jackson finally get the credit they deserve in the scientific community and all across the world.

The moon landing happened just 66 years after the first powered flight.

The Wright Brothers' famous flight took place on December 17, 1903, and it was the first time humans successfully flew through the air in a powered aircraft. (We had used gliders before, but that was basically it.) Just 66 years later, on July 16, 1969, the Apollo 11 mission landed on the moon. Just think about that—lots of people who were alive before airplanes existed lived long enough to see Neil Armstrong and Buzz Aldrin walk on the moon!

Technology advances pretty quickly sometimes, and it's not just planes and rocket ships that can blow your mind. Think about what the internet and smartphones look like today—then ask your parents if they remember having to pay extra for long-distance phone calls!

The first subway system opened in 1863.

London's Metropolitan Railway is the oldest subway system in the world. It was first planned in 1843 and finished in 1863, and it moved passengers from place to place using old-fashioned steam engines! There were vents in the rock to let steam escape, but smoke would still build up in the tunnels and make it hard for riders and conductors to see—not to mention breathe! Even so, people loved being able to get around the city more easily.

In 1890, electric subway systems were invented, and they've stuck around for more than 100 years. Today, just about every major subway system is powered by electricity, either using overhead wires or an electrified "third rail" next to the tracks.

Weird But True!

No one knows who invented bitcoin.

Bitcoin is the most popular (and valuable) cryptocurrency—at least, for now. But the strange truth is that no one is quite sure who invented it. The person (or persons) who wrote the original bitcoin white paper and code went by the name "Satoshi Nakamoto," but it doesn't seem like that was their real name.

Researchers have a few theories about who Nakamoto is, but no one has been able to prove anything for sure. It's too bad—Nakamoto probably owns roughly a million bitcoins, which would make them one of the richest people in the world!

Mobile phones are more common than toilets.

Today, researchers say about 97% of people on Earth have access to cell phones, while just 70% have access to modern toilets and sanitation facilities. That might sound crazy, but it actually makes sense. Indoor plumbing requires a lot of other stuff to support it (like running water, pipes, and water treatment facilities), but a cell phone signal is pretty easy to come by.

Social media started in 1996.

Despite what you may have heard, social media didn't start with Facebook and Twitter. It didn't even start with MySpace. The first social media site was called Six Degrees, and it was launched back in 1996. Six Degrees was the first site that let users create their own profile and connect with other people the way social media users do today. Some other sites have claimed that they came first, but Six Degrees was the first site that today's users would recognize as "social media."

Today, social media apps like TikTok have become a fact of life—so it's interesting to look back on where it all began!

At least 500 hours of video are uploaded to YouTube every minute.

In 2022, researchers found that roughly 500 hours of video were uploaded to YouTube every single minute. That's about 720,000 hours of new video per day! Keep in mind, that was in 2022—which means that number has probably gone up.

That's not bad for a platform originally intended to be a dating website. That's right: When YouTube first launched, the goal was to get users to submit videos of themselves looking for dates!

The company that makes the most tires is . . . LEGO?

There are plenty of companies that make tires for cars and trucks, but the company that makes the most tires in the world is LEGO! Yes, LEGO, the toy maker. The tires that LEGO includes with its toy sets are made of rubber, just like the tires that go on full-sized vehicles, and LEGO makes a lot of them. In fact, they made 381 million tires in 2010, which was far more than any other tire maker in the world. Sure, LEGO tires won't fit on a regular car, but who cares? A tire is a tire!

Mind-Blowing Feats of Engineering

The Roman aqueducts still worked centuries after the fall of the Roman Empire.

One of Rome's most famous engineering masterpieces was the aqueduct. The Romans built thousands of miles of artificial rivers to carry fresh water into Rome and other major cities. These aqueducts were made almost entirely from stone, using very simple tools—even today's engineers agree they are an amazing accomplishment

Maybe the most amazing thing is that the aqueducts were so sturdy and well-made, they continued to work for hundreds of years after the end of the Roman Empire. In fact, the Aqua Virgo aqueduct still functions today—it provides water for the famous Trevi Fountain in the center of Rome.

An iPhone is roughly 100,000 times more powerful than the computer that got us to the moon.

Aboard the Apollo 11 rocket was the Apollo Guidance Computer (AGC)—an incredibly advanced piece of technology for the time. But modern smartphones leave it in the dust! The average iPhone has a million times more memory as the AGC, and it has about 100,000 times as much processing power! The smartphones we take for granted today would have seemed like magic to the scientists in the Apollo Program.

If you think about it, this makes the Apollo Program even more impressive. They managed to land a spaceship on the moon using a computer that most people today wouldn't even be able to use.

Fact or Fiction?

The Hoover Dam is the tallest dam in the world.

Even though the Hoover Dam was the tallest dam in the world when it was built, a lot of even *taller* dams have been built since then. At 726 feet tall, the Hoover Dam is now just the 34th-tallest dam,

Fiction!

while the tallest is China's Jinping-I Dam, which is a whopping 1,001 feet high! Currently, the Jinping-I Dam is the only dam in the world taller than 1,000 feet.

Dams are an incredible feat of engineering. Humans use them to control the flow of water, create artificial lakes, and even change the course of entire rivers! We also use them to prevent floods, store drinking water, and even generate power. The coolest part is that we've been doing it for centuries. The earliest known dam is the Jawa Dam in the country of Jordan, which was built as far back as 3,000 BC. Some of these early dams were built to last: The Sayamaike Dam in Japan was built in the early 7th century, and it's still in use today!

The Panama Canal was built in just 10 years.

Construction on the canal started in 1904, and it officially opened in 1914. Before the Panama Canal, ships had to travel all the way around the southern tip of South America, so it's safe to say people had been looking for a shortcut for a long time. In fact, a Spanish conquistador named Vasco Núñez de Balboa first suggested Panama would make an ideal spot for a canal back in 1513, but it wasn't until the 1800s that anyone actually started to take action.

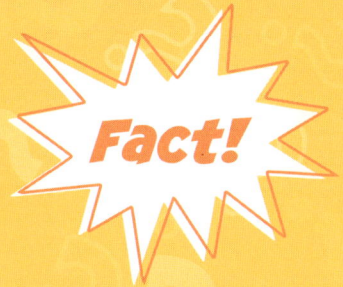

Fact!

France was the first country to try to build a canal through Panama. From 1881 to 1899, the French tried a few times to dig a canal, but it wound up being too expensive and dangerous to complete. In 1904, President Teddy Roosevelt decided that the United States would succeed where France had failed and restarted the project. Ten years later, the Panama Canal was open for business!

What the Future Holds

Artificial intelligence isn't as new as you think.

When you think of artificial intelligence, or AI, you probably think of robots like the Terminator. But actually, the term AI just describes a machine that has even the tiniest amount of intelligence. That means even a simple chatbot technically qualifies as AI—and those have been around forever!

When people talk about advanced AI (the kind you see in science fiction), what they're really talking about is *artificial general intelligence*, or AGI. That's an AI program as smart as (or smarter than) a human. We haven't quite gotten there yet, but some scientists think we're getting close.

Someday, we might power our cities with miniature stars.

The sun's energy comes from something called nuclear fusion. Deep in the core of the sun and other stars, the heat and pressure are so great that atoms "fuse" together into larger atoms—and that releases a *ton* of energy. For years, scientists have been working on a way to create that same reaction here on Earth, and we're getting closer each day. Fusion power would allow humans to use huge amounts of energy without the pollution that comes with other sources like coal and gas. That would help us put a stop to global warming!

Saudi Arabia has a robot citizen.

"Sophia" is a robot created by Hanson Robotics to be as humanlike as possible. She has appeared on television programs like *The Tonight Show*, served as an "Innovation Ambassador" for the United Nations, and spoken at hundreds of technology conferences. She is so humanlike that in 2017, Saudi Arabia became the first country to grant citizenship to a robot!

Despite Sohpia's résumé, not everyone is impressed. While Hanson Robotics describes Sophia as, "basically alive," some critics have labeled her, "a chatbot with a face." Either way, Sophia represents an important step forward for humanlike artificial intelligence.

Acknowledgements

I am grateful to the endless sources of weird and wonderful knowledge peppered across the internet. Researching trivia is always a fun challenge, but it's important to make sure every fact is correct. While I occasionally get things wrong, I try to confirm every fact with at least two sources—and those sources deserve my thanks. So, a sincere thank you to:

- National Geographic
- Nature
- Smithsonian Magazine
- National Public Radio
- PBS
- Encyclopedia Britannica
- Discovery
- Scientific American
- Popular Mechanics
- Popular Science
- Atlas Obscura
- All That's Interesting
- The Secretly Incredibly Fascinating podcast
- The Whippet newsletter
- Snopes
- Wikipedia (always a good starting point)
- ... and countless others

But finally, a thank you to social media posters everywhere. Even facts that turned out to be wrong often sent me down interesting rabbit holes, and for that I am grateful.

About the Author

Shane Carley lives in western Massachusetts with his wife, dog, and flock of chickens. When he was growing up, he wanted to be an astronaut. Now he gets to write about space instead.

About
Applesauce Press
Book Publishers

Good ideas ripen with time. From seed to harvest, Cider Mill Press brings fine reading, information, and entertainment together between the covers of its creatively crafted books. Our Cider Mill bears fruit three times a year, publishing a new crop of titles each spring, summer, and fall.

"Where Good Books Are Ready for Press"
501 Nelson Place
Nashville, Tennessee 37214
cidermillpress.com